HEALING A CHILD'S
HEART AFTER DIVORCE

D1403566

Mid-Continent Public Library
15616 East Highway 24
Independence, MO 64050

*Companion Press is dedicated to the education and
support of both the bereaved and bereavement caregivers.
We believe that those who companion the bereaved by
walking with them as they journey in grief have a
wondrous opportunity: to help others embrace and grow
through grief—and to lead fuller, more deeply-lived lives
themselves because of this important ministry.*

Companion
P R E S S

For a complete catalog and ordering information, write or call:

Companion Press
The Center for Loss and Life Transition
3735 Broken Bow Road
Fort Collins, CO 80526
(970) 226-6050
www.centerforloss.com

HEALING A CHILD'S HEART AFTER DIVORCE

•

100 PRACTICAL IDEAS FOR FAMILIES, FRIENDS, AND CAREGIVERS

•

ALAN D. WOLFELT, PH.D.
RAELYNN MALONEY, PH.D.

Companion
PRESS

Fort Collins, Colorado

An imprint of the Center for Loss and Life Transition

Companion Press is an imprint of the
Center for Loss and Life Transition,
3735 Broken Bow Road, Fort Collins, Colorado 80526
970-226-6050
www.centerforloss.com

Companion Press books may be purchased in bulk for sales promotions, premiums or fundraisers. Please contact the publisher at the above address for more information.

Printed in the United States of America

20 19 18 17 16 15 14 13 12 11   5 4 3 2 1

ISBN: 978-1-617221-42-2

INTRODUCTION

Ideally, childhood is a time in life when we can walk through days without a care in the world. It's a time when we revel in the simple things and discover our world. A time when our only job is to learn, grow, and move toward becoming independent, autonomous souls.

We seldom imagine childhood as a time for confronting and coping with profound loss. Yet each year, this is true for millions of children whose parents decide to end their marriage. Children who go through divorce experience the heartache and pain of "divorce grief"—a distinct grief for a distinct loss.

As counselors and educators, we've had the honor of working with hundreds of children grieving the losses that come with divorce. These children have taught us that every grief experience is unique, and that all children need someone to hear their story and accompany them while they heal from the pain of divorce. We also have firsthand experience with watching our own children grieve, mourn, and heal through divorce.

Divorce grief is not an easy process, but healing after divorce can happen, especially when children have the support of adults who recognize the far-reaching impact of divorce on their lives. Divorce has a way of rearranging the core beliefs that kids have about marriage, love, and family.

Divorce grief is often not seen as real grief in our society. We have a tendency to overlook the reality that divorce is indeed a grief experience, and that the impact of divorce is much deeper than changes in household and daily routines. Children feel every change that takes place, even ones that seem small or insignificant to the adults in their lives. When children go through a divorce, they need adults to recognize the significant impact the experience will have on them today, tomorrow, and always.

The fact that children do not experience loss in the same way as adults complicates their grief journeys. Adults may expect children to cope with divorce in the same stoic, steadfast ways that they do. Mourning the endings and losses associated with divorce is a much different process for children—one that requires our compassionate attention. For kids, experiencing a divorce often feels like the solid ground of their life is crumbling beneath their feet. While adults have the perspective that significant change is often a part of life, kids don't. They deserve a great deal of care and consideration during this time of loss.

Children need us to "companion" them through their divorce grief. To companion means to walk with, to be present to, and to pay attention to what children think, feel, and experience during the divorce process. It means allowing children to teach us what their unique grief journeys feels like instead of telling them what they should or should not feel. It means honoring children and allowing them to feel and express a range of emotions throughout their healing process.

Companioning means witnessing children's emotional pain without trying to take away the hurt or protect them from their own natural feelings. It's hard to watch children suffer, yet if we allow them to feel the pain that surfaces during the divorce process, we help them heal. To companion is to make a commitment to be available to them. To companion, we must continue to be present in the months and years ahead as they experience the wave-like impact the divorce has on their lives.

There are many ways that parents, teachers, and caregivers can help children who are facing divorce. Children respond differently to divorce depending on where they are developmentally (toddlers will naturally respond differently than teens), depending on the nature of the divorce (contentious or amicable), and depending on whether their support system remains intact or diminishes.

Three Factors That Complicate Divorce Grief

Before setting out, it's important to get to know the course. When journeying through divorce grief with children, you'll encounter a few obstacles; knowing what they are ahead of time will help you navigate through them. Consider these three factors:

1. *When divorce occurs while a child is already struggling with developmental tasks*

The primary developmental task for children is to strive toward ever-greater independence. Children naturally separate from their parents and become autonomous as they grow. Separation and autonomy involve relying less on the security of the family and more on one's own sense of security and identity. This process is a normal and necessary part of childhood and becomes increasingly more evident as children enter adolescence. Without separation and individuation, children can't go on to create their own lives, establish their own homes, find their own careers, and have their own children.

Yet during this movement toward independence, children still long to feel loved, cared for, and connected to parents, siblings, and friends. These conflicting goals naturally create ambivalence. When divorce occurs during this period of ambivalence (primarily during the preschool and adolescent years), divorce grief is complicated. Take teenagers, for example. They may unconsciously believe that if they mourn openly in front of their parents, their parents will see them as vulnerable and dependent. For teens, this is incongruent with their strong internal need to move toward, and exhibit, autonomy and self-sufficiency. Teens who put more value on being independent than bonding with the family may postpone their grief and mourning and carry it instead.

As children naturally work on separating from parents, we see them attach more to peers. Friends often become a significant source of affirmation and acceptance for children during late elementary, secondary, and high school years. This, in part, is why children struggle more when divorce interferes with their ability to keep in touch with friends (moving to a new neighborhood, going to a new school, or moving out of state). The loss of friends during the divorce process can be particularly painful for children who developmentally feel more connected to friends than family.

As children move toward independence, they also learn how to self-regulate and cope with their own emotions without help from the adults around them. Divorce causes waves of various emotions, some of which can feel overwhelming to children. Emotions may feel intense and difficult to keep in check. Old ways of coping may not be effective during this time of significant transition.

A child's anger, for example, may feel more intense during divorce because he has many things to feel angry about, but he is unable to pinpoint any of them with words because they are all jumbled together. Anger is a protest emotion. It is his way of saying, "I protest this divorce!" He uses it to vent feelings of helplessness. Anger is a normal grief response, but if he expresses anger in ways that are not constructive (self-damaging or destructive), you may need to seek additional help from a counselor.

It's no wonder, then, that when a child is going through the normal challenges of growing up, and then we pile on divorce grief, it feels overwhelming. Don't be surprised if the child you companion responds to seemingly minor stressors with more intensity or emotionality than usual. For example, she might cry or get angry because she forgot her lunchbox, or she can't get the car door open, or her friend isn't playing with her at recess. Be gentle with her and try not to react to these outbursts with anything but comfort and understanding.

Finally, developmental issues complicate divorce grief over years, not just during the year of the divorce. Children grieve the divorce during a variety of developmental changes. With each stage, their needs and your approach to meeting those needs will change. Children need to mourn the endings and losses of divorce again and again as they develop new ways of thinking about life and relationships. Their divorce grief will surface in different ways and at various points throughout life. Significant events may cause this grief to surface because the events are reminders of the divorce or because the divorce influenced that experience in some way. Sporting events, school dances, recitals, birthdays, holidays, and graduations will all be influenced in some way by the divorce. "Griefbursts"—sudden and unexpected strong feelings of grief— around special events are normal, not only shortly after the divorce but sometimes years later. In fact, many children continue to grieve aspects of the divorce as they enter adulthood and reach other important milestones, such as getting engaged, getting married, and having children of their own.

2. *When the nature of the divorce is abrupt or contentious*

Children's ability to cope well during divorce is directly proportional to their parents' and caregivers' ability to navigate divorce amicably. Children struggle more when they are involved in a high-conflict divorce than when parents work together during and after the divorce to get along and be respectful to each other. The more parents accept and move through the divorce, the more the kids will, too.

Sudden and unexpected divorces create unique challenges for children. Often, parents believe that they only have to sit down and share the news of the divorce with their children once. Yet children do better when the divorce talk is done in doses and continues over time. Too often, the news is shared with children in a way that feels sudden and abrupt. Kids can feel this as true even when parents have contemplated ending the relationship for months or years.

If parents have stayed together unhappily for years, kids may have been grieving the poor relationship, but holding out hope that it would never end in divorce. Often, kids are surprised when they hear the announcement of the divorce, and they refuse to accept it. They feel a need to push away the painful reality that it's finally over, and they may feel choked up and numb that it's really happening. When children have known for a while that their parents were not getting along (overt arguing) or have overheard their parents talk openly about the possibility of divorce, they might express a sense of relief when the divorce finally occurs. Yet relief merely accompanies, rather than replaces, the emotional pain that comes when they are faced with the reality that their family is breaking up and one parent is leaving home. How the news is shared can have a big impact on how kids grieve and mourn.

Because we live in a society that does not always acknowledge that grief is a natural part of divorce, children's grief can become disenfranchised (or overlooked) by others. When children's feelings are disenfranchised, their grief goes unacknowledged. If others refuse to acknowledge that the grief is real, kids, too, will have a hard time believing that it's real and choose to suppress it. Suppressed grief doesn't dissolve. We carry it until we cope with it—now or later.

Disenfranchised grief during divorce can be even more significant for children who are not biological children of the divorcing parents (stepchildren), children who are no longer living at home (college students), or children whose friends and extended family members strongly believe the divorce is best.

3. *When the child's support system is limited*

The quality and quantity of support available to children during the divorce process influences how they grieve. Don't assume that just because children have wonderful families and plenty of friends that they'll have ample support during this transition. It is not unusual for children's divorce grief to go unrecognized, be dismissed, or be set aside by even the most loving adults. Even though children know they have their families, parents, and siblings, they may not want to talk with them about the divorce. Parents and siblings may be less able to offer support because they are overwhelmed with their own grief. This is natural and shouldn't be considered selfish or wrong. However, it does mean that children will need extra support and caring from non-family members during this difficult time.

Children may also lack support when inappropriate social expectations are placed on them. Teens, for example, may be expected to be grown up and lend a hand with younger siblings when the marriage starts to fall apart. Some children are even told that they need to take on more of a parental role ("we need you to be the man of the house"), which can feel overwhelming. When this happens, children do not have the opportunity, permission, or space to mourn the loss of their family.

At times, parents and caregivers assume children will find refuge and comfort in their friends. This may or may not be true. Many children are greeted with indifference by friends. Sometimes, peers avoid talking about the divorce altogether. Unless friends have also experienced divorce firsthand, they do not reach out because they feel helpless or unsure of what to do. Because it's a "downer" to talk about, friends will often ignore the subjects of endings, divorce, and loss entirely when they are together.

Children, especially teens, can be insensitive and at times cruel to those experiencing a profound loss. This insensitivity can happen because it helps teens distance themselves from loss in general. It is not unusual for peers to avoid kids whose parents are going through divorce out of an unconscious fear that divorce might also enter their lives if they get too close. At times, peers may encourage them to avoid or escape their pain and to just get on with life. We call this "buck-up therapy." One of the most influential ways to help children going through divorce is to teach their friends how to be good friends when grief is present. This can be done with simple statements to encourage friends to do the right thing, as in "I'm so glad he has you right now."

How to Use this Book

This book was written to help you companion children through divorce grief. It contains 100 practical ideas for helping children survive, and integrate, divorce. Some of the ideas teach general principles about grief and mourning. Others offer suggestions for activities and guidelines that help facilitate the grief process. While reading, remember that all children will not respond to every idea that's offered.

This book is designed to help parents, caregivers, counselors, and friends and family walk with children as they navigate their way through their grief. Use these accessible ideas to understand how children perceive divorce and what you can do to help them cope. Then, set this book aside and listen with an open mind and an open heart to the children you are companioning. Allow them to teach you what their unique journey through divorce grief feels like for them. In doing so, you will help them release their grief and pain and begin to heal.

Remember, divorce is a shattering experience for children. Their families, as they have always known them, are breaking apart. As a result, their lives are under reconstruction. Consider the significance of the big and small losses that children can feel. Be gentle and compassionate in all your helping efforts. Remember, too, that children do not get over their divorce grief. None of us gets over grief. Instead, our purpose is to help children integrate this experience into their lives, and go on to live with a sense of safety, security, and happiness.

With support and understanding from the adults in their lives, grieving children usually learn that endings and losses are one of the aspects in life that none of us can avoid or control. Kids learn that grief is the natural response to endings and losses, something that they will encounter throughout their life journeys. With loving guidance, they realize that hope and help from others are central to finding their way through loss.

The support you will offer by becoming a companion to the children in your life will help them heal and embrace their feelings, rather than bury them—to live wide open and experience both the joy and sadness that life brings.

Thank you for joining us in our efforts to make a difference in the daily lives of grieving children. We commend you for making this a priority and wish you well as you do the great work of companioning a child through divorce.

Alan Wolfelt   Raelynn Maloney

1.

EXPECT GRIEF.

- Grief is a natural response for all of us when we lose something that we value or feel attached to in some way.

- The child is very much attached to being a part of her family. The family provides a sense of security, safety, familiarity, and belonging for the child. When her family slowly or abruptly breaks apart, she naturally encounters losses as part of that breaking apart.

- Losses may include loss of a family with two parents, what she once felt was her family's home base, financial stability of one family, favorite family activities, and a general sense of being together as a family.

- She needs parents and other adults to acknowledge and give her permission to experience grief when her family begins to encounter the multitude of changes that come with divorce.

CARPE DIEM

Did you ever experience a significant life loss as a child? If so, what do you remember about it? How did it feel for you? Did adults around you acknowledge that it was difficult? Do something today for the child that acknowledges that grief accompanies divorce. Write a note that says, "Sending a hug because it is good medicine for grief" or find some other way to let her know that the feelings she is having are called grief and that they are natural feelings to have during times of loss.

2.

UNDERSTAND THE DIFFERENCE BETWEEN GRIEF AND MOURNING.

- Grief is the word we use to describe the internal thoughts and feelings people experience during a significant life loss. Mourning is the outward expression of that grief.

- All children experience a sense of loss with divorce, but if we want to help them reconcile and integrate that loss rather than avoid, deny, or bury it, we must help them find at least one safe, nonjudgmental space where they can openly mourn.

- While all children experience grief, some children (especially teenagers) work hard to avoid expressing that grief outwardly by mourning. Mourning makes people feel vulnerable and dependent on others, and it is especially difficult when children are moving toward independence and separation as a natural part of their development in adolescence.

- Help the child find safe places to mourn with various adults in his life. It can be you, the parent, a respected teacher or coach, a family friend, or a relative. Ask him which adults he respects and admires in his life. Then talk with these adults and ask if they would be willing to be a contact person for him to talk with about the divorce. If they say yes, have them extend the offer to the child.

CARPE DIEM

Did your parents divorce when you were a child? If so, did you mourn the losses that came into your life openly or did you only grieve, bottling up all of those feelings and carrying them with you into adulthood? If it was the latter, what effect did holding on to those emotions have on your life?

3.

UNDERSTAND THE SIX NEEDS OF MOURNING.

Need 1. Acknowledge the reality of divorce.

• When a child experiences loss, the most important role you play is to help her reconcile the loss and integrate it into her life. Over time, and with the gentle understanding of those around her, she will openly acknowledge that divorce has changed her life course. She will begin to accept that her parents' marriage is ending, her family is changing, and that she feels many losses through the process.

• Do not expect children to acknowledge the reality and finality of the divorce in the same way you would as an adult. Some children embrace the reality slowly and may even seem to feel indifferent about the divorce at times. Others do not experience a full sense of the loss for several months into the divorce process, after the final divorce proceedings, or years later. There is no real timetable to determine when children will feel the full reality of the divorce.

• As you talk with and listen to the child, be conscious of what she's sharing and don't hesitate to share appropriate information with her. She needs to know that what she sees happening is real and what she feels is legitimate. She needs this information, along with loving understanding, to cope.

CARPE DIEM

Today, talk about the reality of divorce with the child. Don't assume that just because she understands what divorce is from an intellectual standpoint that she understands it emotionally. Let her share her divorce story with you in her own words and at her own pace.

4.

UNDERSTAND THE SIX NEEDS OF MOURNING.

Need 2. Move toward the pain of the loss.

- Another important need children have during divorce is to learn ways to embrace the pain of the loss. This need involves encouraging them to embrace all the thoughts and feelings that emerge related to the divorce, even the uncomfortable ones.

- The need to feel the loss is often overlooked by adults. We desperately want to protect children from pain, and we need them to be okay. But the reality is that the only way for children to work through their grief is to go through it—not around it, not under it, and not running away from it.

- Keep in mind that if the child you are companioning seems to strongly resist talking about the divorce, or mourning the losses, this does not mean she isn't hurting inside. It also does not mean she isn't capable of mourning. This response may simply mean she has not found a safe place to be vulnerable, ways to express her grief, or safe people who will give her permission to do her grief work.

- Be patient. If the child does not want to talk about the divorce, don't press it. Just continue to ask how he is feeling about all the changes and offer your support on a regular basis.

CARPE DIEM

Invite her to talk about her family and to tell how it feels to be a part of a divorced family. Be specific. Ask, "What was the best time you ever had with your family when you were all together living in the same house?" Or, "What is something you are going to miss about your parents being married?" Then listen without interrupting.

5.

UNDERSTAND THE SIX NEEDS OF MOURNING.

Need 3. Do memory work.

- Remembering the past makes hoping for the future possible.

- Unlike when someone dies, children who go through divorce do not have a funeral that helps them embrace their memories.

- As you reach out, be creative and spontaneous in finding ways to help the child do memory work. Don't be afraid to flip through photo albums, tell stories, or ask questions. If he has a hard time talking about memories, be inventive. Let him draw a comic strip, write a book, take photos of the family's past homes and favorite stomping grounds for a photo book, make a collage about "family," or have him make a clay model of his family while he teaches you about what this transition feels like for him.

- Sharing memories can be hard for kids because sadness, hurt, or even fear may surface as they share. Some memories will be joyful and funny, allowing them to relive happy times. Others will be painful and may make them cry or express anger. Sharing memories helps kids put together the puzzle of what their family was and what it is now.

CARPE DIEM

Get out your Blackberry, iPhone, or daily planner right now. Find a time each week that you can get in touch with the child you are companioning. How much time you spend doesn't matter. What matters is that you are making contact, and that he has someone who is interested in how he is handling all of the changes. The more time you spend together, the more apt he is to talk with you about the divorce.

6.

UNDERSTAND THE SIX NEEDS OF MOURNING.

Need 4. Answer the question, "Who am I now?"

• Our relationships help us define ourselves. We are someone's child, someone's friend, someone's student, someone's relative, and someone's parent—these all shape a picture of who we are.

• When parents divorce, the child's relationships within the family change. Her relationship with each parent and sibling might change. For example, if she lived with a stepsister before, she may not see her much anymore. Or she may only see one parent on weekends now. Or, her mom might ask her to take on the role of babysitter for her younger brother.

• She becomes a "child with divorced parents"—a new identity for her and one she will now have to carry with her into the world.

• All of these relationship changes can influences how she will answer the question, "Who am I?" For example, her belief that "I am the teacher's pet" might become "I am just one of 500 kids in this new school." Or, her belief that "I am wealthy" might become "I am someone who lives in a smaller home and worries about money."

• Help her define how her relationships were before, and how they are now. Approach it openly, without any hint of judgment or negativity.

CARPE DIEM

Do something physical with the child today. Play catch, go for a hike, bike ride together, or go to the park and swing. After the two of you have had some time together, talk about how she feels she has changed since the divorce, and how those around her have changed.

7.

UNDERSTAND THE SIX NEEDS OF MOURNING.

Need 5. Search for meaning.

- When divorce occurs, kids naturally question what it all means and why it happened to their family.

- Grieving children may ask "how" and "why" questions about the divorce. For example, they may ask one parent, "How can you leave us?" or both parents, "Why can't you get along and stay married?"

- You can help by knowing that these questions are not only normal but important questions for children to ask out loud, even if no one has the answer.

- Though you will be tempted, don't answer the how and why questions for the child. This sharing is about letting him find his own meaning, not imparting yours. It's okay to say that you don't have the answers. You can share that you struggle with the same questions and what you've learned is that nobody has all of the answers. The answers to these questions are inside of him, and it may take some time to find answers that make sense to him. You can acknowledge that it's normal to feel confused, angry, and sad about the divorce.

- Sometimes, children act out their search for meaning in ways that can be dangerous or damaging to themselves and others. While we encourage you not to judge the way your child searches for meaning, self-harming, life-threatening, or violent behaviors indicate that he needs additional help right away.

CARPE DIEM

Ask the child: "Why do you suppose some moms and dads decide to get divorced?" If he asks your opinion, share your beliefs in an open, non-judgmental way to help normalize the situation.

8.

UNDERSTAND THE SIX NEEDS OF MOURNING.

Need 6. Accept and embrace ongoing support.

- The last and perhaps most important need of mourning is to help children receive ongoing support from caring adults.

- Grief is a process that is worked through over time, not an event that occurs at one point in time. Grieving children need support for weeks, months, even years after the divorce because the divorce continues to impact them in various ways.

- Unfortunately, our society places too much value on "moving on," "doing well," and "getting over" grief. Friends and families are well-intentioned by wanting everyone involved to feel better, but often that means they stop calling, coming by, or talking about the painful aspects of the divorce in an attempt to avoid painful feelings. This is often done in place of offering the ongoing support that most families need.

- Children naturally grieve when a divorce occurs. Even after they've worked through some of their initial grief, children may come back to process divorce grief at a later age and work on integrating this loss at a new and deeper level.

- When you can help the child mourn as the need arises (even a year or two after the divorce), you will be helping him integrate this major life transition more fully into his life.

CARPE DIEM

Stop for a moment and think: When was the child first told about the divorce? Has your support for him waned since then? Has your contact been less frequent? Commit right now to contacting or spending time with him on a regular basis so you remain a consistent source of support in his life.

9.

HELP HER TELL OTHERS THAT SHE'S MOURNING.

- Children in our society struggle with grief and mourning. In part, this is because our society doesn't acknowledge that grief is a part of divorce and that family members need to mourn this loss in order to integrate it.

- Children need support and love during this time of significant loss—a time when many of their friends are unaware that they are grieving.

- There are many ways that children can communicate that a significant and difficult life transition is happening in their family. For example, a parent can have the child invite a few friends over for a sleepover and create a subtle theme for the gathering. Parents could talk about the divorce and give each child a bracelet that says a key word, such as *courage* or *strength*, that signifies the transition. Doing so might spark attention from the child's friends, who are given the message that their friend's life has changed. When her friends, teachers, and others see the message, it might remind them to be conscious of this life transition and to be compassionate. If they are observant, they will understand that she needs love and nurturing right now.

- Having an outward sign to tell others that she's in mourning gives others permission to ask her how she's doing. If others don't know, they can't reach out.

CARPE DIEM

Find a way to alert others in the child's life that the divorce is happening. Remind her that if others know about the divorce, they can show that they care through actions and words, and that she will feel more comfortable around them knowing that they know her truth.

10.

MAKE HIS FAVORITE FAMILY MEAL.

• Everything doesn't have to change because the family has gone through divorce.

• Children find comfort in familiar experiences that were part of their family life during the years before the divorce occurred.

• If you are the child's parent, cooking his favorite family meal and eating together (with or without your ex) is a great way to give him comfort and remind him that some things have not changed.

• If you are the child's caregiver, have him over and serve him his favorite meal, or ask him what he enjoyed doing with the family and do this with him. It can be simple, as in riding bikes to a nearby park or playing catch in the backyard.

• These experiences may bring up memories, which might encourage him to talk about what he misses now that his family has transformed.

• Doing something familiar that he enjoys sends the message that these memories and activities can remain a part of his life.

CARPE DIEM

Review the needs of mourning (Ideas 3-8). Which one of these needs seems most prominent right now in the child's grief journey? After doing something familiar together that you both enjoy, offer him help in working through this particular need.

11.

KEEP HER CONNECTED WITH BOTH PARENTS.

- The parent-child relationship is one of the most important relationships in our lives.

- Ultimately, one of the greatest losses children experience with divorce is lost time spent with each parent individually and with both parents together.

- If you are the child's parent, try to put your own feelings for your ex-spouse aside and encourage your children to maintain a relationship with your ex. Don't let your feelings about your ex's behaviors, words, or ability to parent the way you believe is best get in the way of helping them have as good of a relationship as possible. Children deserve to have as many loving, connected, authentic relationships as possible while they are growing up—this is especially true when it comes to parents.

- Remember, when you put down your ex, your child might feel put down too. She knows she comes half from you and half from your ex. Be aware of any indirect messages you may be giving the child about a parent, too—indirect negative messages are at times more damaging to the child.

- Help your child find a way to connect with your ex-spouse or both parents daily.

- As a caregiver, support the child's relationship with both parents. Offer her to use your phone to call, your computer to email, or your supplies to make a card for a parent.

CARPE DIEM

Think about the child's relationship with each parent from her point of view. Set aside your own thoughts and feelings and enter into her world and reality as you consider this perspective. Consider one way you can demonstrate that you support the child's relationship with *both* parents.

12.

USE THE WORD GRIEF.

- Grief is an internal response to loss. Children grieve in their own way, but many show outward signs of grief. These expressions may differ depending on their age. For example, preschoolers may ask the same questions over and over again. Grade-school kids might struggle socially and scholastically or express their grief through acting out. Finally, adolescents might protest by isolating or withdrawing.

- Divorce grief is very real. If you don't see outward signs that the child is grieving, don't assume that he isn't.

- When parents divorce, children experience a multitude of losses. Grief is not limited to the divorce itself; it's also felt as part of the other life transitions that go hand-in-hand with divorce. Children may have to move, change schools, spend less time with one of their parents, split their belongings between two bedrooms, have less financial stability, and so on. All these changes can leave children grieving for the past and the way it used to be.

- Don't be afraid to talk about, and use, the word *grief* with children. Defining grief gives children a word for the strange mix of feelings that are going on inside them—including anger, sadness, hurt, guilt, fear, confusion, and even relief. It may also help children open up because now they have a word to describe what they're feeling!

CARPE DIEM

Ask a trustworthy teacher, friend, or relative who is particularly good at relating to the child to be in charge of giving him extra attention in the coming weeks and months. This kind of one-on-one partnership ensures that he won't be neglected while the family is understandably in turmoil.

13.

REDEFINE FAMILY.

- Divorce is a major life transition for children and their families. Transitions bring up new questions for kids. Some children will want to reexamine their old ways of thinking about family, love, marriage, and commitment.

- The divorce changes the child's definition of family. How she views and talks about family will shift. What she has always known about what it means to be a family is no longer true. Before, family meant mom, dad, and kids living together under the same roof. Now, family means something different and that marriage is no longer a necessary part of being a family.

- Help the child realize there are many kinds of families—some where kids live with just one parent or their grandparents, have stepsisters or stepbrothers, or are adopted. A 2010 Pew Research poll showed that one in three American kids is living with a parent who is divorced, separated, or never married. Take the opportunity to point out examples of non-traditional families.

- Once the idea of family has been redefined and integrated, she will begin to accept this broader idea of family and become more accepting of the way things are now.

CARPE DIEM

Gather photos of the child enjoying herself with each parent. Include siblings, if desired. Put the photos side-by-side in the same frame and present it as a special gift. Write a few lines that describe what was going on the day the photos were taken. Doing so will remind her that even though her family has changed, it is still her family and the important relationships within it are still intact.

14.

REDEFINE LOVE.

- To the child you are companioning, marriage once meant two people who loved each other. With the divorce, he may come to see that there doesn't have to be a marriage for his parents to feel some sort of love for each other and especially for their children.

- You may find that he talks about love and marriage often. This is a part of the redefining process that he is working through. Don't discourage these discussions and wonderings. Encourage the child to express thoughts about love so that you can learn what is going on in the child's mind.

- Help him sort through his feelings by listening without giving opinions as he works on redefining what "love" and "parent" and "marriage" mean now that the expectations, structure, and routines around these concepts are changing.

- Avoid feeding him your definition of love. Part of his grief work is to find his own voice during the divorce process. He'll do so by processing his ideas at his own speed and in his own way. Make sure that he feels your love and caring while he's exploring.

CARPE DIEM

Encourage him to write a letter to his parents about love, telling them what love means to him and how he loves each of his parents. The letter is a form of mourning. It will help him express his feelings around the concept of love.

15.

HAVE AN UNCOUPLING CEREMONY.

- We often use ceremonies to mark significant life transitions. Common ceremonies include weddings, baby christenings, graduations, and funerals.

- Ceremonies around loss help participants convert grief into mourning in the loving and supportive company of others. Through mourning, grief is expressed, embraced, and ultimately healed.

- Ceremony is a great way to help children acknowledge the reality of the changes—both positive and not so positive—that are part of the process.

- The family is experiencing a life transition. Ceremony honors this transition.

- Children may take comfort in seeing others openly acknowledge that the family is transforming and that they are not alone in their feelings.

- There are no rules about what the ceremony must include. It could involve watching old family movies, visiting past homes, going to a favorite spot in nature, or sifting through family treasures. It might involve sharing favorite memories and new triumphs. As long as it in some way recognizes changes that are happening, encourages the expression of feelings, and honors those who are being impacted, it will help the child heal.

CARPE DIEM

As a caregiver, if you don't know all the details of the divorce, learn them today. Doing so helps you better understand the child's grief and encourage mourning. As a parent, stop and consider the journey your child has made with you through this divorce transition. Make a list of the ways you can acknowledge the transition through words or ceremony.

16.

DRAW OR PLAY TOGETHER.

- As adults, we often try to talk to kids about divorce. Yet, talking is not the primary mode of communication for children. Children often express themselves through active play, imaginary play, drawing and painting, or talking to a pet, favorite doll, or friend.

- If you can, connect with the child through one of these child-friendly ways.

- Get down on the floor with him and play with action figures—maybe they are on a mission to save a burning house, or the characters find themselves in the middle of an earthquake. Remember, grief doesn't have to be expressed in words to be released.

- Observe the child you are companioning and find out what works for him. Maybe it is wrestling or singing lullabies that his mom used to sing. Maybe it is pretending to be dad when he's watching football. Capitalize on the type of expression that seems most comfortable for him.

- Encourage the child to draw a picture of "divorce" or create a character out of play dough that looks like divorce. Then let him do whatever he wants with his creation. Let him save it or destroy it; both reactions can be cathartic.

CARPE DIEM

Give the child an open invitation to share with you in whatever way he's comfortable. Remind your child weekly of this open invitation. If you are a caregiver, he may surprise you by calling or emailing out of the blue. If you are a parent, he may start to talk in what seems like odd moments—when you are late to an appointment, right before bedtime, or while you are busy making dinner. Stop and give him your full attention.

17.

CREATE A DIVORCE MANDALA.

- A mandala—meaning circle—is a form of artwork used for meditation. Mandalas originated in the Hindu and Buddhist cultures. Kids enjoy mandalas because they don't have to rely on words to express themselves. Instead, they use color, movement, and visual creativity.

- Download mandala designs online, or, to make a mandala, draw a large circle on a white piece of paper or poster board. Divide the circle into four equal sections and cut out the circle. Get out crayons, colored pencils, paint, markers, and magazines to cut up. Now you are ready to begin. Tell the child that the mandala is to be a picture of her—her thoughts, hopes, dreams, and desires. Suggest that she include favorite colors, symbols, shapes, words, and images. Encourage her to repeat favorite patterns, but remind her that it doesn't have to look like any certain design in the end. Tell her there is no right or wrong way to make a mandala. She can use the whole circle as one space, or take advantage of each section to express something different. If desired, ask her to think about the divorce while making the mandala.

- Let her be in charge of choosing colors and making her design any way she wants. There are no rules for her to follow—just her intuition.

- Mandalas allow kids to put feelings that are buried inside onto something that is outside. This action helps children reconcile grief and actively mourn.

CARPE DIEM

If you want the child to talk to you about the divorce, don't sit her down and ask her questions. This feels uncomfortable for most kids. Instead, take her for a hike, go shoot hoops, or color mandalas together. Action often connects people, making way for meaningful conversations to naturally unfold.

18.

PAINT POTTERY.

- Doing pottery is another way kids can transfer their thoughts and feelings from the *inside* onto something *outside*.

- Visit a local pottery store and help the child choose an object to paint that somehow signifies the transformation that he is experiencing. The child might find a butterfly to symbolize growth, a baby to signify new beginnings, a peace symbol to signify the end of fighting, a dove to signify hope, a car to signify that this is a journey, or a cross to signify the death of something loved.

- The symbolism of the object, and the act of painting it with colors and detail, provides him the opportunity to express himself about how the divorce has changed his life.

- Don't be surprised if you, too, learn something new about how the divorce looks through his eyes.

CARPE DIEM

Today, find out which nonverbal communication style works best with the child. Is he most comfortable when you sit close and make good eye contact? Or is he more relaxed with some distance between the two of you? Does he seem to talk more when you are inside or outside? Be observant and discover which type of setting helps him open up and relax.

19.

MAKE A PHOTO ALBUM.

- Family photos are something concrete that help kids express their families' stories. Each photo often has a story behind it, and looking through photos gives kids a chance to share the stories that they see.

- A part of helping children work through divorce grief involves giving them the opportunity to develop a coherent story about their past, present, and future. This process helps them make sense of their families' journey and the unfolding of their life together.

- Making a photo album gives the child something concrete to work on as she sorts through the emotions of loss and change that come with divorce. It helps reassure her that her family did have some good times, and that there are strong relationships among her and her parents and siblings.

- Emotions that are inside will surface—maybe even emotions that don't seem to come out when you talk. She might talk about what she has lost. Even though this may feel hard, it is healing. It will help her release and move forward with the new circumstances of her life.

- The photo album is something she can come back to when she needs reminding of what her family shared in the past. It can also be a source of hope for what will be shared in the future.

CARPE DIEM

If you are a caregiver, send the child an email today that says, "I just want you to know I care about you and am here for you." Attach an old photo of a meaningful time you two spent together. If you are a parent, take a few minutes and sit down with an old family photo album together.

20.

ENCOURAGE COMPASSIONATE CO-PARENTING.

- When there is tension and angst between parents, children know it. When there is harmony and acceptance, children feel it. This happens even when parents do their best to hide their feelings in front of the children.

- One of the best ways to offer support is to keep your own emotions in check and interact with everyone involved in a civil and respectful way.

- As a parent, demonstrate that even when a marriage ends parents can still get along and work together. They can still say kind words about each other. When you have children together, you are forever linked with your ex. Help your child see that relationship endings do not have to be filled with anger, name-calling, power struggles, and negative energy.

- Consider the good qualities of your ex. There must be something that your ex is doing well around the divorce. Maybe it is being prompt when picking up the kids or conscientious of taking turns with school obligations. Whatever it is, point it out in front of your child. The more your child sees you honestly getting along, the better.

- As a caregiver, if you observe behaviors by the parents that seem damaging, find a good time to gently tell them what you see and how you think their kids might perceive their actions. Offer solutions to ease specific tensions—you might volunteer to help swap kids between homes or help a parent pack during the first few weeks.

CARPE DIEM

Give the child a small journal so she can write down her memories— memories of her parents being together, what it felt like to have them both in the same house, feelings about the marriage being over, and letters to her parents or God about the divorce.

21.

FIND HIM A DIVORCE
SUPPORT GROUP.

- Children need to know that they are not alone when it comes to divorce and that much of what they are feeling is what other kids feel, too.

- If your community offers a group for children coping with divorce, take advantage of it. Groups are a great way to help children feel less alone and different. It's a place where they don't have to feel unique because their parents are divorced—a place where they don't have to worry about being judged or viewed differently.

- Support groups allow children to connect. They give the message that grief over the divorce is natural. They may also provide answers to some of the questions kids have been afraid to ask about divorce. Mostly, groups are a way for kids to meet other kids who are experiencing the same emotions as they are and receive validation that these emotions are normal and okay.

- Groups help kids to not feel so alone in their pain. This can be especially helpful for teenagers who would rather share with peers than adults.

CARPE DIEM

As a caregiver, ask the child open-ended questions about his divorce experience. Then, sit back and listen without too much interjecting. Sometimes questions, fears, and regrets will surface that he has been holding in because he hasn't been asked to share about it recently. Letting him put his experience into words helps him process and can be tremendously healing.

22.

READ A BOOK ON CHANGE.

- Divorce brings about changes that last a lifetime. Some of these changes are experienced on a daily basis, while others are only felt every once in a while.

- Even if children experience other life changes before the divorce (a neighbor moved or the child welcomed a new baby), they may be unaware that change is one of the most natural processes in life.

- A number of books about change are available for kids. Reading an age-appropriate book will help her understand that everything and everyone is constantly changing—nature, the weather, and yes, even families.

- A book about change also gives caregivers and parents a jumping-off point to start a conversation about which changes she feels have been difficult, and which have been easy.

CARPE DIEM

If you are a caregiver, pick up a "just thinking of you" card and write a letter to the child that acknowledges her life changes. Let her know that you care about her with all your heart and you are just a phone call away. Be sure to include your phone number! If you are a parent, slip a similar note in her lunchbox or write a message on the white board in the kitchen.

23.

NOTICE HOW HIS RELATIONSHIP HAS CHANGED WITH HIS PARENTS.

- The child's relationship with each of his parents shifts, even if just a little, when a family is going through divorce.

- The child's parents change as individuals. For example, his parents are now single parents. Both parents may need to work full-time now. Maybe one parent is dating. Parents may feel a greater level of daily stress. When a parent is different, the parent-child relationship will feel different as well.

- Help him acknowledge what feels different now that his parents are separated, living alone, single, or both working full-time.

- Help him find ways to reconnect with each parent based on where that parent is now, not based on where he or she was before the divorce.

CARPE DIEM

If you are a caregiver, stop and send the child's parents an email that says, "I just want you to know that I think (child's name) is a great kid!" Back it up with a recent example of something you observed the last time you were with him. If you are a parent, plan a special outing or activity to reconnect with your child on a one-on-one basis.

24.

MAKE A FAMILY MEMORY BOX.

- The child has cherished memories of being a family. There are probably many activities, places, and items that trigger these memories. Some of her memories are happy, some sad, and some may not stir many emotions at all.

- If your child is a collector, this idea may be especially helpful to her. Take some time to help her collect objects that represent family memories. For example, maybe the child will choose a rock from the backyard of the family home, last year's Christmas letter, a shell from a beach trip, a photo of a family vacation, a picture she drew of the family when she was young, or a Lego because the family used to build Legos together. Whatever the child decides to put in the box is fine.

- If desired, help her make a personal box for her items. She can decorate it with her favorite symbols—hearts, peace signs, animals, or whatever—and add drawings of her family. Have attractive ribbon and colorful pieces of patterned paper on hand to make the box special. If making the box isn't possible, supply a unique box for her treasures.

- Ask her about each item and why she chose to include it.

- She can pull out her items when she's missing her family or is feeling the need to express emotions about her loss.

CARPE DIEM

Look up the family name and jot down the meaning. Write a note explaining the meaning to the child and tell her why it's a great name, no matter what changes are happening in the family.

25.

ACKNOWLEDGE HOLIDAY GRIEF.

- No matter what time of year the divorce occurred, when the holidays come around the reality that the family is apart and the new parenting schedule reminds children that their family has changed.

- Children might experience waves of emotion during the holidays because they are reminded that many things are different: holiday plans, family traditions, the family home, and mostly that the family is no longer together as one unit—the biggest change of all.

- As parents, it doesn't matter if you warned the child that the holidays were coming and that they'd be different; feeling the change is entirely different than being told about it.

- As a parent or caregiver, you can help the child by acknowledging the reality that the holiday is different. Let him voice his sadness or disappointment. Honor his feelings with a special gift and note. For example, find a special ornament that signifies change or have an ornament made for him that will remind him of his family as it was in the past. Attach a note that says, "I understand this new way of doing things is hard for you."

- Giving a gift that acknowledges his pain helps him express how things feel strange and unnatural, allowing you a chance to provide comfort.

CARPE DIEM

As a caregiver, ask the child if he has holiday photos of the family and if he would share them with you. If you have photos of him and his family from past holidays, share them as well—he may have never seen them before. Use this opportunity to start a conversation about his family—how it was then, and how it is now.

26.

FIND A MARRIAGE MEMENTO.

- As parents, if you are not sure what to do with your wedding ring or wedding band after the divorce, consider gifting them to your children.

- You can also take both rings and have them melted together, reshaped, and transformed into a piece of jewelry that can be given to your children. A gift like this is deeply meaningful. It is symbolic of the dissolution of the marriage (when the rings are melted), the ongoing connection between her parents (the rings are now one), and the new beginnings that she will experience (the rings have a new shape or form).

- Other marriage mementos might include items from the wedding day, such as a veil, gloves, silver goblets, dried flowers, a copy of the wedding video, and photos. As parents, consider placing some of these items in special boxes and giving them to your children when it seems appropriate.

- If you are a caregiver who attended the wedding, share photos of the parents' wedding. Talk about your experience and observations of the wedding day.

CARPE DIEM

Today, talk to the child you are companioning about collecting keepsakes that represent the family and her parents' marriage. If she has already selected some that are important to her, ask her about their significance. If she hasn't found any yet, help her find at least one.

27.

TALK ABOUT DIVORCE
IN KID-LANGUAGE.

- Some children send a clear message that they do not want to hear the word divorce or talk about it with adults. Children might bury their heads in their hands when someone talks about divorce or change the subject immediately when it comes up in conversation. This is often because adults have demonstrated "not talking about it" very well.

- It's possible to help a child work through his avoidance. First, be sure that as an adult you feel comfortable talking about the divorce and observe whether or not you are talking about it in his presence. If you're not, he might get the message that divorce is a taboo topic. If you are, he'll be more likely to open up because you're giving the message that it's safe to do so.

- Keep in mind that children tend to come up with their own language around divorce, and sometimes this makes it easier to talk about. Whether they talk about you getting "unmarried" or say there is a "divorcement" in the family or refer to it as a "break up" or focus on dad's or mom's "move out," children are teaching you the words that makes sense to them. Use this language when communicating with the child.

- Don't be afraid to talk about the divorce. Sometimes we think if we don't talk about it, we'll avoid upsetting the child. The truth is he carries thoughts and feelings about the divorce with him, constantly.

CARPE DIEM

Choose a book on divorce and ask if you can read it with him. There are several books on divorce—both in story form and as workbooks. Two good books include: *Families are Forever* by Craig Shemin and our book *Healing After Divorce: 100 Practical Ideas for Kids.*

28.

EASE THE TRANSITION
BETWEEN HOUSE STAYS.

- Children of divorce often undergo transitions every week and sometimes every day. In general, transitions can be hard for kids.

- Certain days of the week are more emotionally challenging than others, such as the day the child transitions to the other parent's house. She has settled in at one house, and now she must let this comfort go and shift to the other house. Weekends and holidays will also trigger extra emotions.

- Help the child prepare for these difficult days in advance. Talk openly and ask how she is feeling about the holiday that's coming or going to her dad's house for the weekend. Let her know that it's okay to have feelings about how the divorce changed things for that day, suggesting that kids in her shoes often feel sadness, anger, confusion, frustration, and sometimes, relief. Emphasize that all of these feelings are natural.

- Encourage her to bring a favorite item back and forth—a stuffed animal, blanket, or special pillow—so she doesn't have to leave all of her items of comfort behind. As a parent, sneak a note in her pack that says, "Enjoy your time with mom. I'll see you again soon."

- One of the best ways to ease transitions, as parents, is to keep calm and positive during the exchange. Avoid telling your child that you will miss her. Worse yet, never ask her to report back on how mom or dad did over the weekend.

CARPE DIEM

Brainstorm ways the child can create a sense of continuity during transitions. Make a special necklace that can serve as a touchstone or create a button of a favorite family picture for her travel bag.

29.

"LISTEN" TO HIS BEHAVIORS.

- Children often communicate emotional turmoil through their behaviors rather than words.

- Because children don't have the vocabulary to articulate complicated feelings very well, they often express much of their mourning through behaviors and actions.

- Watch and listen for telling behaviors. Rather than telling you, "I feel really sad right now" the child might withdraw, get quiet, or whine more often. Rather than saying, "I am really angry with my mom for moving out," he might act out aggressively at school or throw more tantrums at home.

- Help him find safe physical ways to express his feelings. Have a swordfight with foam swords or play a game of tag with squirt guns. Best yet, have his family join in so he feels their acceptance with his behavior.

CARPE DIEM

Compassion literally means "with passion." Care for the child with passion today—do an activity together that lets him express his strong feelings.

30.

REMEMBER, CHILDREN HAVE RIGHTS.

- Adults usually have attorneys, judges, and therapists reminding them of their rights during the divorce process. Keep in mind that the children have rights, too.

- Children have the right to express their authentic feelings even if what they are feeling or thinking is not pleasant for parents to hear. Children have the right to openly talk about any issue they want with both parents. They should not be expected to keep something secret from one parent because the other thinks it will cause trouble. Children also have the right to connect with both parents every day, even when they are splitting their time between parents.

- As a caregiver, teach the child that she has rights and help her communicate to her parents that she deserves to have these rights upheld.

CARPE DIEM

What are your strengths? Your weaknesses? Take an honest assessment of your own strengths and limitations to determine how you can best help the child during this process. Bank on your strengths and choose ways to share them. Maybe it's your ability to show empathy, experience joy, or listen well.

31.

AVOID SECRETS.

- When families live in separate houses, parents sometimes inadvertently encourage their children to keep what happens at mom's house at mom's house and what happens at dad's house at dad's house. Without realizing it, parents are asking their kids to keep secrets. This makes kids feel like they must live two separate lives. If the secrets are contentious, it makes them feel like they are the rope in a game of tug-of-war.

- Asking kids to keep secrets puts too big of a responsibility on them and distances them from both parents. It also teaches them to relate disingenuously with their other parent and others.

- Even though the intention behind the secret may seem good (you don't want to upset the other parent, for example), it gives the message that they can't talk about their life with each parent. This creates angst, confusion, stress, isolation, and fear.

CARPE DIEM

Make a list of divorce and counseling resources within your community, including the name, location, time, phone number, and cost. Give this list to the child's parents or to an older child who can make the call himself.

32.

GIVE HER A LOCKET.

- A locket is symbolic. Think of it as a vessel that carries hope or a place to put her pain. It is carried close to the heart—and right now her heart might feel broken or bruised.

- Lockets hold objects that people find meaningful. They can hold photos, quotes, dried flowers, and more.

- When you give the locket, tell her what it symbolizes. Maybe you put in a picture of her family to remind her that they are all still in her life, and that she is still connected to them. Maybe it's a piece of beautiful, silk cloth to remind her that there is beauty in her life—and that a future of rich experiences awaits.

- For boys, consider a an engraved pocket watch. Better yet, find a small, silver container that can be carried in his pocket.

CARPE DIEM

Ask the child to talk about the locket or pocket watch and what it means. Doing so sends the message that it's okay to talk about the family and the divorce—which helps the child to heal.

33.

HAVE A MOVIE NIGHT.

- Plan a night to watch a movie together. Choose a comedy so you can share a laugh and lessen the load, at least for a few hours.

- If you want, facilitate healing by selecting a movie with a divorce theme. Consider:

  - *Mrs. Doubfire*
  - *Tender Mercies*
  - *Kramer vs. Kramer*
  - *Irreconcilable Differences*
  - *War of the Roses*
  - *Micki & Maude*
  - *Kids & Divorce: For Better or Worse* (documentary)

- You don't have to talk about divorce before, during, or after the movie. The purpose is to connect with the child, be present, and send the message that you understand the divorce is hard for him and to show him that divorce is a part of life.

- By spending time with him, you are letting him know that he's important to you.

CARPE DIEM

Buy him a copy of the movie you watched together or download the soundtrack onto his iPod or MP3 player. It will remind him that he's not alone in divorce.

34.

GET A GIFT FOR EACH PARENT.

- Children know divorce is hard on their parents. They see the emotional toll divorce takes on each parent, and they feel bad about it.

- Help the child pick out a meaningful gift for each parent. This has a dual-purpose: it helps her acknowledge that others also feel pain from the divorce and demonstrates thoughtfulness and compassion toward others. It also helps her acknowledge her own grief in the process.

- Help her find a gift that has meaning. Maybe it shows tenderness toward her parents' pain or communicates that even though the family is separated, they are still a family. Consider:

  - Candles and bath salts, scented shaving cream, or other self-care items
  - Flowers to symbolize harmony, hope, and love
  - Mood rings that change colors
  - CDs with songs that remind her of good times with her family
  - Framed photographs of her and each parent

CARPE DIEM

Ask the child: if there were no limits on cost or size, what gift would you give each of your parents? What gift would you want from them? What gift would you give yourself?

35.

USE SOCIAL MEDIA SITES.

• As a caregiver, family member, or friend, stay connected to both parents and the child regularly via social media sites. Send pokes and quick messages to let them know that they are on your mind. Offer your help and support.

• If he doesn't have one already, help the child set up a site—of course check with his parents first. Help him link up with friends, cousins, other relatives, and both parents to create a social network of his own.

• Try Facebook as an easy introduction to social media. Teach him how to accept and reject friends and to safely use the internet.

• Some sites are specifically designed to help divorced families stay connected and communicate with less conflict—such as Ourfamilywizard.com and Divorce.com. These sites help parents schedule shared and joint custody exchanges and communicate over other issues in a non-combative way.

CARPE DIEM

Right now, search to see if the child already has a Facebook or Myspace page. If so, look over the content and invite the child to be your Friend. Of course, as a responsible parent, you will want to monitor the child's Facebook or Myspace pages.

36.

DON'T SHATTER HOPE.

- When parents divorce, their kids inevitably wish and hope for them to reconcile. Because getting divorced is a huge decision, parents feel its finality and the truth of it. They want to share this truth with their kids—stating loudly and clearly that they will never get back together.

- While telling kids the truth is good, this news can feel more like shattered hope. As parents, keep in mind that your kids' hope is a natural response to divorce and that it will likely diminish as they absorb the reality of the divorce.

- Instead of insisting on being direct and final about the divorce, dose your kids with information. Dosing means spreading information out over time and giving just what's needed to satisfy a question.

- Avoid creating false hope by saying that maybe you'll get back together when it doesn't feel true. Rather, when they ask, you can simply say that right now, this is the decision you two have made.

- Take a realistic look at your kids' ability to cognitively and emotionally process the divorce. Accept that your kids might not be in a place to accept or embrace that there is no hope right now. If you give information slowly over time, they'll be better able to absorb it.

- If you are a caregiver, share with kids only what they need to know about their parents' divorce, leaving out the unpleasant details.

CARPE DIEM

Give the child a hope rock. Garden and novelty stores have rocks with words carved into them; often you can find one with the word hope.

37.

WAIT TO INTRODUCE
NEW PARTNERS.

- It's hard for kids to accept that the marriage is over—and nothing brings this home faster than when a parent gets involved with someone new.

- Experts advise waiting one to two years to introduce a new partner to kids after divorce. Children need time to absorb the reality that the marriage is over and get comfortable with their new life of visits or sharing homes.

- Young children feel confused when new partners are introduced. They can also feel threatened—believing the new person will take priority in their parent's heart and that they'll have yet another loss— their parent's time and love.

- As a parent, when you introduce a new partner, do it thoughtfully and slowly. First, have them meet on neutral ground. Resist showing too much attachment and emotion to your new interest. Be conscious to give your children a lot of attention during the meeting, sending the message that even though this new person is here, they'll remain your top priority. Don't expect your child to fall in love with the person, too.

- As a caregiver or friend, reassure the child that love is not finite— parents can love someone else and that doesn't mean they will have less love for her.

CARPE DIEM

Give the child an "*I am here for you*" card. Use your business card and write in big letters "I am here for you" on the back. This lets her know that you are on-call when she needs to talk. Deliver the card in-person or mail it to her. Kids love to get mail!

38.

FIND SPACE TO MOURN.

- It's important for kids to express their grief—and all the feelings that come with it—outwardly through mourning. They can do this with safe people and in safe places.

- Some children feel embarrassed or vulnerable expressing emotions, especially if they witness the adults in their life stoically "carrying on" after divorce.

- Help the child identify with who he feels comfortable sharing his emotions with. Go through his list of friends, teachers, relatives, coaches, school counselors, faith-based caregivers, and pets. Remember, it must be his choice, not yours. Send an email or make a quick call to the adults he chooses to put them on alert that they're on his list.

- Journals also offer safe places to mourn, as do sketchbooks.

- If he names you, let him know that he only needs to tell you what he wants, when he wants, and that you won't push him to talk.

- Sometimes kids need a physical, sacred place to mourn. When death occurs we often go to the cemetery, but with divorce there is no set place. Help him find his own place—maybe you two bury something in the garden and mark it or create a shrine in the corner of his room. You could also find a thought-provoking spot in his neighborhood or at a nearby park, like a fallen tree or a pond's edge—anyplace he can go to sit with his feelings.

CARPE DIEM

Fill a small bag or basket with treats and snacks and leave it for him in his safe space. Include a note that says, "Take your time."

39.

DON'T TRUST THAT SHE'S OKAY.

- Kids often try to take care of people around them. If parents give cues that they need them to be okay, kids will often act okay.

- Don't be fooled. Kids are never okay with divorce. For kids, their entire foundation—and all they've ever known—is their family, the way it was. When divorce happens, it feels like an earthquake that leaves grief and loss in its wake.

- Parents hate to see their kids suffer—especially when they feel like they had a part in causing that suffering. Inadvertently, parents can send the message that they don't want to hear about their kids' feelings.

- Perk up when the child says she is okay with the divorce. What she may really mean is that she wants to avoid or deny the pain it brings. Or, she doesn't feel safe to share her feelings about the divorce with her parents, family, or friends.

- Explore with her whether or not she thinks it's okay to talk about the divorce. Tell her that burying feelings doesn't make them go away. They remain in us until we let them out.

CARPE DIEM

Buy or make a dream-catcher for the child. Suggest that she hang it above her bed or in a window in her room. Explain that dream-catchers are believed to catch bad dreams and that the morning sun burns them away.

40.

FIND A KEEPSAKE.

- Kids are drawn to trinkets and keepsakes. Help the child find one that reminds him of his family before the divorce.

- Give him ideas, or take him shopping at area gift stores. Consider:

    - Glass or clay figures of animals that form a family
    - Snow globes or national park trinkets that remind him of a past family trip
    - Books he had when he was little that he remembers his parents reading to him
    - Collections of rocks, marbles, or jewels, with one for each member of his family

- Keepsakes like these serve as physical reminders of what his family was like before the divorce, when everyone was together. When he picks up his keepsake and looks at it, it helps him integrate the idea that the family he had is no longer the same, that it's now a memory.

- It's good for him to remember, reflect, and feel what his old family life was like. Ironically, it helps him accept his current situation a little more easily.

CARPE DIEM

As a parent, write thank you notes to all the adults who are helping your child right now. By affirming their support, you'll keep the support coming—something he needs right now.

41.

TAKE CARE OF THE FAMILY PET.

- Pets are proven to bring healing and calm. Studies show that our heart rates lower and our moods improve when we spend time caring for and stroking a pet.

- Help the child connect to her family pet right now. By giving to another, she'll gain strength herself.

- Kids often feel helpless during a divorce. When they are responsible for another creature, and carry out their responsibilities, they gain a sense of control in their lives.

- Help the child develop a routine or plan to make sure she has opportunities to take care of the pet through food, attention, treats, and walks. If you are a parent, reassure her that when she is away from the pet, you'll take good care of it.

- If she transitions back and forth between two homes, help her stay connected to the pet when she's at the other house. If you are a caregiver, offer to pick up her dog and bring it with you on an outing. Or, give her a photo of her dog that she can carry with her between houses.

CARPE DIEM

Get the child a stuffed animal that looks like her real pet. She can pack it in her bag when she goes to her other parent's home.

42.

MAKE A FAMILY COAT OF ARMS.

- Children typically keep their last name after divorce, even when a parent doesn't.

- A coat of arms is a symbol that depicts the family's cultural heritage. Sometimes, coats of arms can be found by searching the last name on the internet or researching it in a book. If you find one, print it out in large format for the child to color and decorate.

- If a real coat of arm doesn't exist, make one. Get a large sheet of cardstock paper and draw the shape of a shield. While looking through a book for ideas, sketch out symbols and shapes that appeal to the child or let him do it on his own.

- This activity will help him maintain a feeling of belonging to his family despite the divorce.

- Consider symbols that show strength—lions, tigers, a giant tree, and others to instill a sense of family pride and represent a strong family bond.

CARPE DIEM

Let the child hang the coat of arms in his room. If possible, have it embossed on his backpack or made into a patch that he can put on an item that he carries between houses.

43.

ENCOURAGE FEELINGS.

- Help the child identify and own his feelings. Sometimes, what he's feeling is not always clear. Kids are loyal to their families and can take on feelings that their parents have or feel what they think they should feel rather than their true emotions.

- Let's say the child is bitter toward his father. He might project this bitterness onto his siblings. Authentically, however, he might feel a strong need to talk with or see his father to resolve unfinished business.

- Pay attention to what's going on with the family and identify any feelings that are being displaced or projected. Let him know it is okay to feel differently than his siblings and parents and that only he knows how he feels.

- Be ready for strong feelings that he might have toward one or both parents for making the choice to get divorced.

CARPE DIEM

Help the child take a break from his feelings. Take him to a toy store to check out the toys or go to the park and play tag on the playground. Play helps to open hearts and reveal true feelings.

44.

KEEP FAMILY PHOTOS.

- Some parents throw out family photos, believing it's better to get rid of reminders of how the family used to be. Their intentions are good—they are trying to protect their children from pain—but they don't realize that they are actually causing more harm than good. Parents are actually sending the message that it's better to not feel pain, yet to heal from grief you must feel it.

- As parents, keep in mind that getting rid of keepsakes like family photos is like burning part of your child's history. Photos are part of your child's family story and family heritage. Don't take that away from her—they serve as stable ground when she's feeling shaky and help her maintain her self-identity through the divorce.

- If you are a caregiver, encourage the child to share family pictures with you and tell you her memories.

CARPE DIEM

Contact relatives and gather photos of the family the child has never seen before. Ask them for a brief description of when the photo was taken. Gather these photos into an album for her to keep.

45.

GIVE COMFORT WITH LINKING OBJECTS.

- Linking objects are objects that bring the child comfort and remind him of things that he's lost. A linking object can be anything that has meaning to him—the key to the family home, a well-worn stuffed animal or blanket, a piece of jewelry, a baseball, a parent's wedding band, a knickknack from a family trip, and so on.

- Give the child permission to carry the object around so that he feels comforted by it throughout the day. As he holds the object he'll be reminded of the reality of his loss. This is good as it helps him separate what was from what is—and begin to accept that his life has changed.

- Help kids understand how linking objects help them when they are having a hard time.

CARPE DIEM

Invite the child to visit a pediatric unit of a nearby hospital. Take a few stuffed animals for her to give out to the children staying there. By sharing a linking object, she'll find extra comfort in her own.

46.

REMEMBER THE OTHER PARENT.

- Children need each of their parents for different reasons. Even if the divorce was contentious between parents, the child needs both of her parents in her life, when possible.

- Each parent brings something different to her life that the other cannot. Mom and dad have unique influences on her sense of self-worth, coping skills, and gender-identity.

- Even if a parent did something viewed as terrible or parents are not on speaking terms, fostering some sort of positive interaction between the child and her other parent will help her create a story about this transition that helps her integrate her divorce grief. Maybe contact has to be limited to letters, emails, texts, phone calls, or supervised visits—but these connections, however limited, should be maintained.

- Keep in mind that children love unconditionally. Even in turmoil, they still desire to stay connected to both parents.

- As a caregiver, support the child's relationship with both parents by talking about each in positive terms and asking her to share her feelings and memories about each parent.

CARPE DIEM

Observe the mourning style of the child's family. Gently
suggest family counseling if you think it would help.

47.

MODEL RESPECTFUL, POSITIVE BEHAVIOR.

- Children who experience divorce often observe contention and animosity between their parents. Some overhear conversations where a parent—whom they love—is being bad-mouthed and judged. Others have a mom or dad who directly shares negative opinions about their other parent. This doesn't feel good to kids no matter what has happened because they value a relationship with both of their parents.

- Be one of the adults in the child's life who demonstrates that relationships, even when an ending is near, do not have to be filled with animosity and negativity.

- Model for him that even when people disagree or have strong feelings between them, they can still interact with maturity, rationality, and compassion.

- If you are a parent, let your child see that you can and will communicate with your ex-spouse in a respectful, polite way. If you need to, limit interactions to just business or use texts or email to communicate to avoid talking if you can't get along right now. Avoid talking badly about your ex, even when he or she gives you reason to do so.

- If you are a caregiver, speak about both of the child's parents in a positive way.

CARPE DIEM

Give the child a packet of Pop Rocks candy and teach him about how energy feeds off other energy and can be positive and healing or negative and dividing. Encourage him to recognize when he is taking on someone else's energy and to consciously decide if he wants to adopt that energy as his own. Ask him which people in his life have positive energy and encourage him to spend time with those people—especially on hard days.

48.

TALK TO THE TEACHER.

- When parents divorce, some children don't share the news with anyone, even those they see on a daily basis. It's important that people—like teachers—who are a part of the child's social circle know the family's situation.

- If you are a parent, call the school and ask to talk with your child's teacher. If your child is in middle school or high school, ask to talk with the school counselor, who can pass the news on to her teachers.

- If you are a caregiver, encourage the child to share the news with her teacher and school friends. Explain that she doesn't have to share painful details if she doesn't want to, but letting others know helps them be able to offer support.

- Don't assume that she will share the news with trusted adults in her life. She might, but she also might feel like it's a private matter or that it's too painful to bring up. As a parent, you could join your child in meeting with the teacher.

- Sometimes, divorce affects kids' school performance, motivation, focus, and behavior. The child naturally is going to be more distracted and may feel more emotional. When emotions surface at school, she might not know what to do to cope. It helps to have caring adults who can offer understanding and comfort.

CARPE DIEM

Right now, call the child on her cell phone or reach out and gently touch her to let her know that you are thinking of her. Tell her you just wanted to check in and see how she's doing.

49.

TALK TO THE SCHOOL COUNSELOR.

- Children don't always know who to turn to when they need support.

- School counselors are great resources and can keep a caring eye out for your child. School counselors are especially trained to help children cope when they are going through difficult life transitions.

- As a parent, talk to the school counselor about your divorce and share how you think your child is coping. Share how he is struggling and identify ways he needs help right now. Tell how he best accepts support.

- The counselor may be available to meet with your child one-on-one, if needed. He or she can also communicate with teachers and staff that your child interacts with—sharing a plan on how to best support him.

- It's a good idea to check in with the counselor regularly. If your child is facing an especially difficult event—like mom or dad moving away—let the counselor know. Also, if your child seems especially out-of-sorts one morning, let him or her know that as well.

- As a caretaker, encourage the child to talk with the school counselor. Reinforce that counselors are often good listeners.

CARPE DIEM

Sit down with the child and develop a list of people who listen well—people he could turn to if he needs to talk about the divorce. Explain that talking about the divorce and sharing his feelings will make him feel better. Let him come up with the list, but make sure that you and the school counselor are on it.

50.

PRAY.

"What do I pray for?" There are two kinds of praying: For purpose and for object. The first is concerned with the reason for praying while the second involves what the prayer asks for. The first recognizes that all prayers have intention and the second that all prayers are petitions."

–Joe B. Jewell, *The Elements of Prayer: Learning to Pray in Real Life*

- Prayer is an important way to maintain faith, whether the faith is based in religion or in the idea that life contains goodness and hope.

- If the child is religious, help her tap into her connection to God through prayer. Prayer often brings respite from grief and pain.

- Children need answers to sort through the grief and pain that divorce brings. Religious and spiritual beliefs can be a source of comfort and bring peace and hope.

- As a parent, introduce the idea of prayer to your child—if you haven't already. Help her figure out what to pray for by having her voice what she would like to have happen in her life. Help her identify specific things to ask for to make that intention happen. Have her pray for people she loves.

- Avoid making promises that prayers will come true. If she asks, tell her prayers might come true, but not always in the form that we want or recognize. Explain that praying is not just about asking, but about us understanding what we want and need, too.

CARPE DIEM

Give the child a copy of your favorite prayer that you learned as a child. Share with her how you've used this prayer and how it helped you when you were feeling down.

51.

TALK ABOUT MARRIAGE.

- Because a child is experiencing the end of a marriage, the child might feel the need to talk about marriage in general terms. Explore the idea of marriage with her.

- What she knew about marriage has changed. Help her make sense of the change. For example, she may have believed that marriage was supposed to be forever. Help her realize that all marriages do not last and that some people get married more than once.

- Explore the concept of marriage through words and physical play. Ask questions to help her express herself. If she's young, play house with her with dolls or action figures, or use another avenue to create pretend play about marriage.

- Divorce naturally makes children question and wonder—as all major transitions do.

- Give her the space she needs to explore her ideas without giving answers based on your own personal beliefs. It may take her time to integrate her changing ideas about love and marriage.

CARPE DIEM

Let the talk about marriage come as naturally as possible. When she brings it up, explore her thoughts with open-ended questions, like "Why do you think that's true?" or "What do you think about that?"

52.

FIND KIDS WHO'VE BEEN THROUGH DIVORCE.

- When big losses happen in our lives, we often feel alone in our pain. Help the child feel less alone by introducing him to other kids who have been through divorce.

- Brainstorm with the child about kids he knows at school, on his team, or at his church who have divorced parents. Suggest that he could talk with these kids about their experiences with divorce.

- As a parent, talk with your divorced friends and ask if they would feel comfortable playing a role in helping your child through this time. Also ask for tips in helping him cope with divorce.

- As a caregiver, ask a divorced friend or neighbor if they would share their story with him so he can gain perspective on divorce—and see that it happens to other people, too.

CARPE DIEM

Plan an evening of fun with the child and other
friends who have also experienced divorce.

53.

BE PRESENT.

- The tricky part of divorce is that parents are grieving, hurting, and overwhelmed, which makes helping their grieving and hurting kids even harder. Understandably, people get consumed with the challenges that come with divorce. The result is that parents can become emotionally unavailable to their kids—leaving them feeling confused and alone.

- Be an adult who is available and present to the child not only physically but also emotionally.

- Being present means you are living and breathing in that moment with the child. You are consciously not letting other things (stress, anger, tiredness, bitterness) get in the way of being fully there in heart and mind. You lose yourself in the present moment.

- When you are present, she knows that you are listening. She knows that you are paying attention. She feels that you are in tune with her life and feelings.

- When children experience stressful life changes, they need to know that there are adults who are available, who care what they have to say, and who have the capacity to be actively engaged.

CARPE DIEM

Live in the moment with the child. Take her on a hike. During the hike, stop and observe the sights, sounds, and smells around you. Literally stop and smell the roses, touch the grass, or listen to the birds. Being in the moment will help you both feel calm and centered.

54.

GIVE A HUG.

- Most kids love physical affection, even teenagers who appear to not want it. As a parent, offer hugs often, but don't force your child to hug you. Make time to take her into your lap or sit next to her on the couch and simply hang out without talking.

- Physical affection says *I accept you, and I know what you are going through is difficult and that you deserve love and support.*

- As a caregiver, before you give a hug, read the child's body language— are her arms crossed or is she hugging herself tightly? Or, does she appear relaxed? Make sure she's comfortable with this expression of love and support.

CARPE DIEM

If you can afford it, splurge on a massage for the child. If she has never had one, tell her what it's like and that getting a massage helps your muscles and mind relax. If you can't afford it, offer to rub her back or massage her shoulders, if she's comfortable with it.

55.

LET HIM CRY.

- As adults, we often want to prevent kids from crying. It's hard for us to see kids in pain, and their tears make us uncomfortable.

- Crying is a natural physical response to feelings of sadness and helplessness. Crying is a way to bring what's inside, out. Once released, tears often bring some relief from pain.

- When we cry, our breathing slows and makes us feel calm. We feel a physical release of emotions.

- Let the child know that it's okay to cry. Boys especially need to hear this message.

- Rather than trying to comfort by saying, "Shhhh, don't cry, it is okay," simply sit with him and rub his back. The divorce doesn't feel okay to him, and you don't have to make it okay. Letting him feel what he's feeling will help him move toward acceptance.

CARPE DIEM

Box up a linen handkerchief and present it to the child with a note that explains that crying when we're sad helps us feel better.

56.

MODEL MOURNING.

- Children learn by example. When it comes to grief, children learn by watching how adults mourn during divorce.

- As a parent, be a model mourner. Let your child witness you expressing emotions to others. Reach out to show her that it's important to seek support from other people.

- If you tend to keep your feelings inside, she might feel less comfortable letting her own feelings flow when she's with you. If you avoid the topic of divorce, she will too. Your actions teach her what's taboo and what not to talk about or express. If you show emotion openly and talk about the changes that your family is going through, she will be more likely to talk freely about them as well.

- By mourning well, both kids and adults can live well and love well.

CARPE DIEM

Write a poem about grief or find one that you like. Share the poem with the child and start a conversation about why it's important to mourn when you feel grief and sadness about things that happen in life.

57.

VISIT THE OLD HOUSE.

- With divorce sometimes comes moving. If the child is no longer in the house he lived in with his family, help him remember the old house. Encourage him to talk about it and reminisce.

- As parents, it's tempting to avoid driving by the house. It seems easier to leave the past behind. Trying to forget won't help your child accept the change that's happened in her life, though.

- The house or neighborhood itself may have felt like an anchor to her. Now, she's trying to establish that same feeling of being grounded or anchored in two new homes. This takes time.

- If she misses the house, it's okay to drive by or even walk the neighborhood. Let her emotions surface and listen to what she misses about the old house or neighborhood. Facing these feelings head on—even when it doesn't feel great in the moment—helps her integrate the reality that moving was one of the losses she experienced with the divorce.

CARPE DIEM

Help the child connect to her new neighborhood(s). Find nearby parks, bike trails, and playgrounds. Locate the nearest movie theater and mall. Do something fun at one of these locations to start building new memories.

58.

TALK ABOUT BOTH PARENTS.

- With divorce, kids' worlds become divided. There's mom and then there's dad. What was once integrated is now separate—but kids still need both parts.

- It's important that the child be encouraged to talk about both of his parents. As a parent, if he hears you talking about your ex in a neutral or positive manner, he'll feel freer to talk about him or her as well.

- As a parent, have you formed a silent agreement with your child that you won't talk about your ex when you are together? Maybe this wasn't intentional, but because of hard or uncomfortable feelings between you and your spouse, the message was inadvertently given to your child.

- Keeping your spouse out of the conversation is unnatural, since he or she is still a major part of your child's life. It's akin to not talking about school, a huge part of your child's day.

- As a caregiver, if you have negative feelings toward one or both of the child's parents, set your feelings aside and ask him about each of his parents. Keep the conversation as positive as possible—giving the message to him that his life is not broken, and that his family, although different, is still important.

CARPE DIEM

Find a coffee house that features lives music. Go with the child and listen to music, sipping hot chocolate. Talk about his parents and tell him what you like about each of them. As a parent, think of a few positive things you can share about your ex-spouse, or discuss neutral topics about your ex.

59.

REMIND HER THAT
PARENTS ARE FOREVER.

- Divorce changes many things, but one thing it doesn't change is that parents always remain parents to their kids.

- As a parent, tell your kids, "I'm always going to be your mom (or dad) whether or not we stay married, and I will always love you." This may seem obvious, but it is reassuring for kids to hear.

- As a parent or caregiver, let the child know that you will always be there for her. Be sure she knows she can count on you.

- Stop and listen and look into her eyes when she talks. Purposefully spend time with her—doing things she enjoys. As a parent, doing so gives the message that although there are many changes, the fact that you are parent and child is not one of them. As a caregiver, you'll send the message that you are another solid adult in her life.

- Don't make empty promises. If you commit to being there, show up. Now, more than ever, she needs you to be reliable. If you can't, apologize in a heartfelt way and set another date up immediately.

CARPE DIEM

Sit down and look through the child's baby book with her to show her that no matter what happens with the divorce, she is always going to be that child who was born to the two parents in the picture.

60.

WRITE A FAMILY EPITAPH.

- An epitaph is a "short text honoring a person who has died" and often appears on the gravestone. It often expresses love and respect for the person. When families divorce, children often feel as if the family is dying or has died.

- Help the child express this and mourn openly by writing an epitaph or obituary that helps him communicate about his experience of loss.

- Develop one on your own or use the one that follows. Let him fill in the blanks to express his thoughts and feelings:

On _____(date of divorce or separation) the _____(family name) family experienced a divorce. It left the children feeling _____. The cause of the divorce was due to _____. What will be missed the most about this family living together is _____ and _____.

- Ask him what he'd like to do with the epitaph. He could put it in his journal, make a cardboard frame for it and include a family photo, or simply post it on his wall.

CARPE DIEM

Take the child to a cemetery to gather ideas for an epitaph.
Have him bring paper and pencil to copy down his
favorite epitaphs that he reads on the gravestones.

61.

PLAN A SPECIAL DAY.

- Now more than ever, the child needs time with loving, caring adults. Plan some quality time where it is just you two. Do something where you can focus on being together and enjoying each other.

- Pick something she enjoys or something that you two have enjoyed doing in the past together. Maybe it is taking a hike, going to the zoo, playing a board game, or floating on inner tubes at a nearby lake.

- Let the child know that you want to spend time with her because you understand that this experience with the family is hard. If you are a parent, tell her that you believe it's important to find ways to stay close while the family goes through this change and that when she feels a need to have one-on-one time, she should let you know.

CARPE DIEM

Search the local paper or phone book for museums, galleries, or farmer's markets. Or peruse the entertainment section for upcoming community events. Choose one or two that you think will appeal to the child. Ask her to join you for the event.

62.

BE HIS ADVOCATE.

- If you notice that the child is struggling but the other adults in his life don't see it, commit to being his advocate. Advocate by letting others know his needs—what he tells you and what you see.

- Sometimes, parents get overwhelmed and become blinded by their own needs and are unable to handle their kids' needs, too. Gently remind mom and dad that the child needs them right now and offer to do tasks or errands to free up their time so they can spend time with him.

- Advocate for him by being a present, loving, and supporting adult. Offer to be his voice if he feels he can't share his needs himself.

- Explore the different areas of the child's life with him. Listen for things he feels are unfair, frustrating, or difficult. Maybe he's having a hard time meeting the demands of his football coach or is having trouble getting long-term school assignments done. Ask him if you can help him work these issues out with his coach, teachers, parents, or instructors.

CARPE DIEM

If the child has missed some school or is struggling, help him stay on top of things by picking up homework assignments and delivering them to the house. Offer to help with homework if you can.

63.

TELL HER IT'S NOT HER FAULT.

- Kids of divorce tend to play the "if only" game in their minds. They might think, "If only I listened better or didn't get into trouble, maybe mom and dad wouldn't have fought so much and wanted a divorce." The end result is that they can and often do find a way to blame themselves for the divorce.

- If you are a parent, let your child know that she is a source of joy in your life and had no part in why you and your spouse decided to split apart. Remind her in doses that you and your ex both are responsible for the divorce. Divorce is due to parents' behavior, not kids' behavior.

- As a caregiver, remind the child that her parents decided they couldn't live together and that had nothing to do with her.

CARPE DIEM

Spend time with the child this week. Plan a project the two of you can work on together, like making a bulletin board or finding a small table or bench for her room and painting it.

64.

MAKE A VISION COLLAGE.

- Vision collages help us put our hopes and visions for the future on paper. They remind us of what we want in our lives, helping us subconsciously—and consciously—work toward them.

- Get a stack of magazines, glue, scissors, and poster board for both you and the child. Spread out your supplies and start cutting out pictures that represent what you'd like to see in your futures—smiling families, skydiving, a new kitchen, traveling, whatever appeals.

- Don't worry about talking during the process—if it happens, great, if not, no worries. You'll learn a lot about what he's thinking from the pictures he chooses. If desired, talk about your vision collages when you're done—starting with yours to get the ball rolling. If he doesn't share, take it as a sign that he'd like to keep it private, at least for now.

CARPE DIEM

Give the child an art basket that has all the materials he needs to draw, paint, and create art on his own. Go to an art store and pick up a sketchpad with colored pencils, markers, or crayons. Include a glue stick, tape, and colored and decorated paper. Put everything into a basket, wooden box, or closable file folder. If desired, add yarn, googly eyes, stars, stickers, and other craft items.

65.

LISTEN TO HER FAMILY STORY.

- When something happens that's unexpected or significant in our lives, it's cathartic to tell the story to other people. Telling the story helps us to integrate what happened into our lives. It gives us a chance to make sense of it as best we can and recognize feelings that we have about the occurrence.

- When we face major changes, we can feel shock. The child might have felt shock when her parents told her about the divorce—and if it is still early on she may still feel shock. While shock helps us protect ourselves when pain is too great, eventually we need to move through the numbness and denial that it brings.

- Encourage her to tell her family's story, including the divorce, in spoken words, acting, pictures, or writing.

- As the child tells her story, don't feel like you have to correct her if you remember it differently. She's telling it from her perspective.

- As she tells the story, be curious, be present, show interest, and bear witness to her truth.

- After some time has passed, ask her to share her story again. Children's divorce stories evolve as they move through mourning. By listening to her story over and over, you'll help her heal and grow.

CARPE DIEM

Give the child a "Publish Your Own Book" kit. She can use this to write her family's story, if she wishes, or write another story altogether.

66.

ENCOURAGE JOURNALING.

- Some children like to put their feelings or thoughts into words. If the child likes to write, consider buying him a journal.

- Take him to the store and have him pick out a journal. Ask if he'd like one with a lock or without. Also, buy him a fun pen or set of colored pencils to go with the journal.

- Encourage him to think of a title for his journal and to write about his feelings around the divorce and what his life feels like. The title could be something like: "My Life During the Divorce" or "My Family is Changing."

- Ask if he'd like to integrate family photos into his journal. If so, help him gather them and copy them, if needed.

CARPE DIEM

Write a note in the front of the journal that tells your feelings of admiration for the child. Describe who you think he is, in detail. For example, you could write "To Owen. You are one of the most talented kids I know. You really know how to go for it in soccer and in life. You have a great smile. Keep showing it to the world."

67.

SEND A CARD.

- Children love to get personal mail. It's a special treat that makes them feel important.

- As a caregiver, send a "Just Thinking of You" card with a personal note.

- As a parent, slip a note into your child's lunchbox or tape it on the bathroom mirror. Tape it on the door, or sneak it into his coat pocket. It can simply say, "I am so glad you are my kiddo."

- If you want, acknowledge the challenges of the divorce. Don't be afraid that you'll bring up sad thoughts—he carries sad thoughts already. The note is simply your way of inviting those sad thoughts to momentarily surface in the context of your support. This reminds him that he's not alone in his sadness.

- Consider writing something like: "This divorce thing is the pits. Don't you think? I hope you have a good day even though things are not easy right now. I care about you very much!"

CARPE DIEM

Make a custom postage stamp for the child that has a picture of his family on it, and use it when sending your card. (Check out postage stamp-making websites like www.photo.stamps. com or zazzle.com.) Put a few extra stamps in the envelope for him to use for times when he needs to send a letter.

68.

SEND A CARE PACKAGE.

- Children need to feel cared about, especially when they go through major life transitions.

- Sending a care package is a great way to remind the child you are thinking of her and that you care about her.

- Include items that you know she likes and needs. These personal gifts will remind her that you know her well and help her feel like she can rely on you.

- As parents, consider making a care package together for her—one that she can take to one of your new homes. By making it together, you are giving her the message that you both stand together to support her, even if you are not remaining married.

CARPE DIEM

Include a nightlight in the care package. They come in all varieties, from stained glass and ceramic to plastic designs and shells. Pick one you think she would like and include a note that says, "Wishing you peaceful nights and restful sleep."

69.

FRAME FAMILY PICTURES.

- Family photos are important reminders to children that their family is whole, even if they live in different houses.

- The photo will remind the child that he belongs to his family, then and now. If desired, make a photo collage that includes photos of both the past and present—including ones recently taken in his new house or individually with each parent.

- Help him find a place to hang the photo where he can see it regularly.

CARPE DIEM

Ask the child to make a list of the top 10 things he likes to do with each parent. Make a copy and send the list to each of his parents, letting them know that their child loves them and would like to spend time with them doing the things on the list.

70.

PLANT A GARDEN.

- Gardening has a way of nurturing feelings and bringing peace. The idea of growing plants from seeds or watching tiny plants become strong and produce fruit is not only satisfying but a symbol of hope and growth.

- If you like to garden, include your child in this activity this spring. Give her a plot to cultivate and let her decide what to plant and where to place her plants. Call it her healing garden.

- If you want, have her pick a plant that represents each family member.

- Tending to her garden might help her work through feelings about the divorce or at least bring her peace in an indirect, nurturing, and playful way.

CARPE DIEM

As a caregiver, give the child and her parents gardening gloves. Put a note on the gift that says, "Keep your family growing strong through this time of transition."

71.

TALK WITH—NOT AT—HIM.

- Often as adults we rely on words to get an important message across. Yet using words is an adult way to communicate; words don't always register with kids. Kids don't always take in what you want them to take in, and the message sometimes gets jumbled into something you didn't intend.

- To communicate more effectively with the child, talk *with* him, not *at* him. This means having a two-way conversation in which both of you are sharing back and forth. The alternative feels more like a lecture, where you talk and he listens.

- Talking with him means he's a necessary part of the conversation.

- A good trick to talking with someone is to speak from the "I" versus the "You" point of view and asking open-ended questions. For example, saying "I feel like the living room looks messy when we leave our stuff lying around. What do you think? It makes me feel disorganized and grumpy. I would like it if we both tried harder at putting our things away when we come home from school and work." This is much different than "You always drop and leave your backpack and shoes on the floor when you come home. You need to pick them up."

- Talking "with" helps him feel connected and heard because you are interacting. The alternative leaves him feeling disconnected and defensive.

CARPE DIEM

The next time you're with the child, remember to use the "Teach Me" principle of learning about grief. The Teach Me principle is essentially taking the time to let the child teach you what his experiences are like without interrupting, giving your opinion, or trying to correct him.

72.

CONNECT EVERY DAY.

- Children who feel connected to their parents are less fearful and anxious, especially during major life transitions. When they are connected to others, they feel a sense of safety and security that makes all the difference when facing major life challenges.

- Consciously create moments where you and the child are connecting intellectually, emotionally, physically, and spiritually. For example, play games together, write notes to one another, explore or read together, and pray together.

- Life gets busy, especially during the week. As a parent, even setting aside just 30 minutes for direct, eye-to-eye, fully engaged contact a day will be enough to keep you two connected, helping her to feel secure. Plan weekly get-togethers where you can devote a few hours to just being together.

CARPE DIEM

Make a list of seven ways you can stay connected to the child, one for every day of the week. If you are a caregiver, your list might include phone calls, texts, notes, emails, and hand-written notes on days you can't get together, with a planned weekly outing.

73.

ACT IN HIS BEST INTEREST.

- As parents of divorce, we can get lost in expressing our own grief, pain, and anger about the divorce and lose sight of what effect our words or actions might be having on our kids.

- Adopt a practice of consciously pausing and asking, "Are my actions helping or hurting my kids? Are they making my kids feel secure or unsettled?" Consider the idea of parenting from your "highest self." In other words, step outside yourself in a situation and ask, "What would my highest parent do in this situation? What is my best response? How do I want to respond or act?" Often, this pause and looking toward the best response helps us be the parent we want to be.

- Don't be afraid to get an objective opinion from someone else (a counselor, for example) about whether your decisions or actions are in your child's best interest. It's okay to acknowledge that your perspective may be clouded by your emotions right now.

- As a caregiver, consciously check how you talk with the child about the divorce and his parents. Make sure that you remain positive or at least neutral in your opinions.

CARPE DIEM

Take a few minutes right now and do an internet search
with the keywords "children's rights during divorce" or
"children's feelings about divorce" to get a clearer view on
what the child might be feeling during this trying time.

74.

BE SILLY.

- We all need breaks from our emotions and thoughts during times of change. Just because the child is going through something serious doesn't mean she has to be serious about it all the time.

- Sometimes humor about a trying situation is more healing than words and deep discussions. When we laugh about divorce, it can make it easier for kids to digest and open up and talk about it.

- If the child makes a joke or tries to use humor to cope, support her. She is exploring ways to release her pain.

CARPE DIEM

Get the child a joke book. Sit with her today and read jokes together or share ones of your own. Laughing builds intimacy, connection, and feelings of hope for a happier future.

75.

WATCH FOR WARNING SIGNS.

- Sometimes, kids in distress act out aggressively or inappropriately to get attention. They can also become overwhelmed and stop functioning well—slipping with personal hygiene, schoolwork, and staying connected with friends. Even more concerning, they can become depressed and stop doing things they like. They might perform poorly, withdraw from others, and show other signs of depression.

- Warning signs also include sadness, excessive worry, self-harming behaviors, trouble with peers, and struggles with school. If you are seeing these over time, consider counseling.

- All kids struggle with divorce. There is no way around it, and pretending they are fine doesn't help matters. Ask yourself, "Do I need him to be fine?" If the answer is yes, know that he is ultimately paying a price for acting the part. Acting fine when he's not teaches him to bury and stuff his feelings. Sometimes, these feelings will then surface as anger or inappropriate behaviors. If stuffed for a long time, they can affect his future relationships. Even though it is hard to hear him talk about his pain around the divorce, do your best to open up and invite him to do the same.

- Even if you are not seeing anything unusual, know that he's grieving.

CARPE DIEM

Right now, make a list of concerns you have about the child based on his behavior. As a parent, address them. As a caregiver, gently share your concerns with his parents.

76.

HELP THE FAMILY MOURN.

- As a friend or relative of the family, you can support the family by acknowledging that divorces are difficult, especially if the family doesn't want to talk about it.

- Find ways to give this message—that divorces are hard—followed by an offer of help in subtle, caring ways. You can send a card to family members with a note acknowledging what they are going through, give the child a coloring book about divorce, offer to make dinner and bring it to their house, or send a plant with a message of encouragement and support.

- Watch for opportunities to help the child release her grief when you are together. Be open to talking about her feelings, even the difficult ones. Consider ways to release her emotions through play, ceremony, talking, and art. Helping her move through her emotions of grief will ultimately lead to acceptance of them, releasing her from constantly feeling despair or pain.

- Know that grief is not something kids or their parents will "get over." But when they face it and walk through it, they'll integrate it in a way that makes sense in their lives. You'll know they are making progress when they are able to talk about it openly and do things that remind them of being a family without experiencing painful emotions.

CARPE DIEM

Prepare a meal for the child and her family. If possible, suggest they all eat together, like old times, with you (if desired) as the server who pampers and caters to them.

77.

DON'T DISENFRANCHISE THE CHILD'S PARENTS.

- To disenfranchise a person means "to deprive a person of a privilege or right." There are many subtle ways that divorced parents are disenfranchised by friends, families, and relatives.

- Because they are no longer a couple and are now single, certain invitations stop coming. Couple friends might stop calling either parent, or call just the one to which they feel the closest. If the link was family-based, as with school friends, people might stop inviting the family to outings, feeling it would be awkward to do so.

- Be conscious of this fact; offer support and extend invitations and leave it up to them whether or not to accept. Consider what they had before that they've lost because of the divorce. Maybe you can extend your help—offer to take care of the kids, make meals, or clean the house. Doing so will provide them with time alone or a night out with friends.

CARPE DIEM

What is the child's favorite dessert? Buy the ingredients and help him make the dessert to give to each of his parents.

78.

SET UP A COUNSELING APPOINTMENT.

- When we are going through intense personal changes, it helps to have the objective eye of a third party. A counselor can provide a different perspective on the situation—seeing ways to support the child that may have been overlooked.

- When picking a counselor, take time to make a good match. Visit a few to find one that the child connects to and who makes her feel safe. Ask others who have been through counseling for suggestions.

- Explore resources in town for families going through divorce—especially if money is an issue. Remember that the child can see her school counselor, too.

- Ask the counselor if he or she has experience working with kids who are going through grief after divorce. Even good counselors can sometimes overlook the grief a child feels and become more focused on making the divorce logistically work for everyone.

CARPE DIEM

Share with the child your idea of what a counselor is like.
Mention that the counselor is there to support her and help
her feel better inside and that the counselor is someone who
often helps kids who are going through divorce. If you've
seen a counselor yourself, share your experience of how you
were helped. Tell her what to expect during the visit.

79.

CONSIDER HIS AGE.

- We assume that younger children are less vulnerable to or affected by divorce. While younger children may show fewer outward signs of struggle, this does not mean they are unaffected. Even infants feel changes in their parents' emotional states. Toddlers understand the absence of one parent and may express anger and a desire to see that parent. They may revert to old behaviors (having accidents, using a pacifier) or start having nightmares.

- Preschool and elementary-aged kids know that divorce means their parents will live apart and that they no longer love each other the way they used to. They may blame themselves and worry about changes in their daily lives.

- Pre-teens and teens understand what divorce means but may fight accepting it. Teens might feel abandoned, express anger, and act uncharacteristically.

- Kids of every age are affected by divorce. Giving each child—regardless of age—extra attention, reassurance, and stability is important during this time.

- Be aware that as kids grow their reaction to the divorce will change.

CARPE DIEM

Connect with the child at bedtime tonight and let him
know that you are glad he's in your life. Call, or if you
are the parent, sit at his bedside. Tell him, or write a note
telling him, what he brings of value to your life.

80.

GO THE DISTANCE WITH GRIEF.

- Children don't get over divorce. They can integrate it and come to a place of acceptance, but it will always be a part of their personal stories.

- It's easy to want kids to face the divorce, adjust, and be finished with it. Instead, as caregivers and parents we have to be willing to go the distance with the kids in our lives. We need to check in with them as they grow and as the years pass—and as kids experience their new and changed feelings about the divorce at different ages and stages.

- At each developmental stage, kids will ask new "what ifs" and "whys" as their ability to critically think, reason, and cope with emotions expands.

- Revisiting her experience will help the child fully integrate the divorce into her life, limiting the negative effects it could have on her future relationships and beliefs about love and marriage.

CARPE DIEM

Sometimes, seeing things that are larger than life helps us gain perspective. Get online or call your local extension office to figure out when the next meteor shower will occur. Invite the child to accompany you to watch it. Pick a spot that provides a great view. Bring goodies and blankets and plan to stay up late watching this amazing phenomenon together.

81.

LIMIT CHANGE.

- Right now, stability and a predictable routine is what the child needs. Whenever possible, keep the number of changes in his life to a minimum.

- The more changes he has to encounter, the more disruptive the divorce process will feel. If possible, keep him in the same house and at the same school, so his day-to-day routine doesn't change much. If that's not possible, make changes slowly and one-at-a-time to help him adjust better.

- As a caregiver, help him feel secure through these changes by doing things that are familiar to him. If he always goes to a nearby park to shoot hoops, do that with him, even if it's not the closest park now. If he plays soccer with the same kids each year, let him join that team again.

CARPE DIEM

Brainstorm a list of changes the child has gone through since the divorce. Consider how you would feel if that many changes happened all at once in your life. Most likely, you'd feel a loss of control. Ask him to read the list and add to it. Doing so will reassure him that others recognize the hard changes in his life.

82.

CONSIDER WHAT KIDS NEED.

- Kids experiencing divorce tend to need the same things.

- Kids need parents to stop fighting—especially in front of them, and especially about them. When parents fight about kids, kids tend to feel guilty or think that they did something wrong.

- They need both parents and meaningful adults to stay involved in their lives. When parents stay involved—even it it's only through emails and texts—kids get the message that they matter and are loved.

- Kids need both parents to raise them. They don't want to take sides or be put in the middle between parents.

CARPE DIEM

As a parent, ask yourself honestly how you are doing in regards to the above list of kids' needs during divorce. Pick one concrete way that you can improve. As a caregiver, think about ways you can support the parents in getting along or spending time with their kids—maybe offering to take the child out so the parents can talk over issues privately.

83.

THINK ABOUT HER CULTURE.

- Children are products of their cultural environment. Culture permeates all areas of our lives—how we communicate and how we view the world.

- The way the child expresses grief and how she seeks help with her grief are influenced by her culture. Some cultures promote expressing emotions openly. Others promote being stoic and holding in emotions.

- Some cultures cope with loss with the help of their religious communities. For example, many people who were raised Catholic may use prayer as a way to cope through loss and difficulties.

- As a caregiver, respect the child's cultural background and consider how it is influencing her grief process. Explore with her how people in her family and extended family express emotions.

CARPE DIEM

Think about your own cultural background and how it influences your life. How has it influenced your thoughts and beliefs about divorce? Ask yourself, "How can I best respond to this child's unique cultural background?"

84.

AVOID SENDING MIXED MESSAGES.

- As parents, when emotions are running high we're more at risk of sending mixed messages to our kids.

- Mixed messages come when our behaviors don't match our words. For example, you might say, "The divorce is not your fault" to your child but your behavior (being unavailable and distant) might say something else. He might get the message that you're angry with him and that he did something wrong. He could even jump to the conclusion that if he were a better kid, you wouldn't have gotten divorced.

- Explain your feelings and reactions. If you let him know your anger is not about him, he'll be less likely to take responsibility for your actions and feelings personally.

- Be careful to not live hypocritically. Watch out for times you are living the proverbial "Do what I say, not what I do." For example, if you scold your son for fighting with his brother but then turn around and fight with your ex, you're acting hypocritically.

- We all let our emotions get the best of us at times. Don't judge yourself; just do the best you can to repair it. An honest apology or recognition of what you did wrong with your kids goes a long way in healing imperfect parenting moments.

CARPE DIEM

Give the child a voice-changer—a toy that makes his voice speed up, slow down, and change pitch. Use it to help him know that you are aware that adults, like the voice-changer, can give mixed messages that make no sense and sound wrong. Tell him you want to be an adult who doesn't do this. Give him permission to tell you when you're words, actions, or messages are confusing.

85.

KEEP STRESS IN CHECK.

- Divorce brings stress and strain to everyone involved, particularly when the divorce is contentious.

- When we are feeling stressed, our stress trickles into how we interact with our kids—even when we think we are hiding it well.

- As parents, when we feel heightened stress we become more reactive, overall. Sometimes this translates to reacting in anger or frustration over something our kids do, when normally we wouldn't respond in such a way.

- When you are interacting with the child, be consciously aware of the stress and tension you feel and separate it out before engaging with her.

- If you don't realize your mistake until after, make sure you let her know you realize your reaction wasn't appropriate so she knows your stressed response wasn't because of her.

- Remember, she is also feeling heightened stress and turmoil and may also be reacting more to what's happening in her life. Go easy on her when she overreacts, helping her sort through her own feelings.

CARPE DIEM

How does the child cope with stress? Make a list of five specific ways to help her cope with stress. Tell her "Let's get out some of that stress that's bugging you." Then, do something with her to release it. Physical activity, and conversely, relaxation are both great stress relievers. Consider a list that includes items like: 1. Running around the bases of a baseball diamond, 2. Playing tag, 3. Building a sand castle, 4. Breathing in fresh air, or 5. Taking a long, hot shower or bath.

86.

SHOW WHAT RESOLUTION LOOKS LIKE.

- When children witness resolution, they learn how to resolve conflicts. Conversely, when they witness conflict without resolution, they learn to hold grudges.

- If the divorce is wrought with conflict and the child is witnessing much of it, try to be the adult who models proactive communication by actively working to resolve conflicts in a fair, compassionate way.

- When you can't demonstrate resolution, at the very least talk with the child about what you wish you could do to resolve a situation. Focus on the ideal, positive outcome without saying anything negative about the person you are in conflict with.

- Model non-grudge-holding to the child. The next time you are in a situation that triggers an old grudge, respond to it differently. Make a conscious choice to thoughtfully respond rather than react.

CARPE DIEM

How can you help the child know that where there is anger, there is still love? Find a creative way to show him that this is possible. Reassure him that when you are angry about something he did, you don't stop loving him.

87.

AVOID EUPHEMISMS AND CLICHÉS.

- When loss occurs friends and family often fall back on euphemisms or clichés in response to their loved one's pain or grief. People say things like, "You'll get over it," "Time will heal," or "Let it go."

- The reality is that these pat responses don't help the child feel better. Instead, they tend to minimize her response to the divorce and encourage her to deny her feelings of grief.

- Avoid saying things that make it sound like divorce is easy. For example, she won't feel better if she hears: "It'll all be fine. Lots of families get divorced." Or, "This isn't the worst thing that could happen." And, "Things are going to be better this way."

- Instead, try to imagine what it's like from her perspective—that the one, unshakeable thing in her life, her family base, is now crumbling at her feet. Know that it will take time to rebuild and give heartfelt, honest acknowledgment of her pain.

CARPE DIEM

If you've used any of these phrases, don't worry too much. The child knows you are trying to help. Make a concerted effort from this day forward to avoid clichés and euphemisms as you work to support her.

88.

SURF THE WEB.

- Take some time to scour the internet for helpful information about kids and coping with divorce.

- There are many kid-friendly websites with lots of interesting information about how divorce feels for children. For a list of the top ten, visit www.lovetoknow.com/top10/children-of-divorced-parents.html. The link to www.kidsturn.org offers pages for kids with suggested activities, artwork, and articles.

- By seeing that others experience divorce, the child may feel less alone in his experience and realize that divorce (although hard) is not something that is happening to him alone—as kids tend to feel when they are going through this difficult life transition.

CARPE DIEM

Offer a simple yet powerful gift to the child—give him permission to mourn. Let him know that it's okay to mourn in your presence. Tell him he can share or express any emotions he is having right now, and that it's okay with you. Create opportunities for this to happen. Reassure him that it's normal to feel a lot of different feelings—even ones that are opposites of each other.

89.

MAINTAIN FAMILY RITUALS.

- Just because the marriage ends doesn't mean that certain family rituals have to end, too. The more you maintain family rituals, the more you help the child maintain a sense of safety, security, and connection.

- As a parent, consider established rituals that you've had over the years around holidays, and think of ways you can maintain these. Also, consider less-established rituals, like playing family baseball in the park, family game night, or Sunday football game parties. Can you keep these alive, even if they need to be modified?

- Of course, some rituals will change. Maybe the guest list will be different, or maybe it will include just mom or dad and not both. Maybe it's no longer dad who leads the Thanksgiving prayer or reads the poem on gratitude—it's now grandpa. Yet keeping the basics of the ritual alive helps kids feel like their lives are secure and predictable.

CARPE DIEM

Review ideas 3-8 in this book on the needs of mourning. Which of these needs seems most prominent right now in the child's grief journey? Brainstorm ways you can help her work on this need.

90.

FEED HER BODY.

- Get down to the basics—make sure the child's basic needs of eating nutritiously, sleeping well, and exercising are being met. Keeping her body running in its best condition helps her to better cope with stress and the onslaught of emotions she's feeling.

- It is not uncommon for kids to lose their appetite or have sleep difficulties during significant life changes like divorce.

- Be conscious of feeding her healthy, well-rounded meals. Consider dividing the dinner plate into four parts—fill two parts with vegetables, one with grains, and the last with meat. Offer her fruits and vegetables regularly, sneaking them into snacks with carrots and dip and ants on a log (celery, peanut butter, and raisins). Try to get her to eat five fruits or vegetables a day by keeping a conscious daily count.

- If her appetite is low, encourage it by making her favorite meal or letting her pick out new fruits or foods to try at the grocery store.

- As a parent, be a good role model for self-care by eating well, exercising regularly, and having good sleep habits. Practice good sleep hygiene by getting to bed at a regular time each night, not exercising right before bed, doing relaxation or calming activities before bed, and keeping the room dark for sleeping.

CARPE DIEM

Pack a picnic basket with a healthy lunch or hearty snack and take her to the park for a picnic. If the weather doesn't cooperate, have the picnic inside on a blanket on the living room floor instead.

91.

ENCOURAGE TRUE FEELINGS.

- Allow the child to feel whatever he is feeling when he's thinking about something he's lost due to the divorce. It's tempting to try to fix his loss by filling it up with gifts or encouraging him that it's not all that bad. That's not what he needs. He simply needs to be listened to, heard, and understood.

- No two children will have the same emotional experience of divorce, including siblings. Try not to force your ideas of what he should feel on him. Practice acceptance. Bite your tongue if needed and remember this is his reality he's sharing, not yours.

- Kids commonly experience shock and numbness when they first hear about the divorce and during the coming weeks and even months. We can't rush them to integrate the reality of the divorce or hope they accept it and move on. Yes, they will eventually settle in to the fact that their parents are divorced, but in their own time.

- Challenge yourself to sit with his emotions, even the hard ones. Worries and fears can become more pronounced in children when they are going through a lot of changes. Anger is also common, as are hurt, helplessness, and confusion. Be mindful of this fact, and consider ways he is expressing these emotions.

CARPE DIEM

Read a book about feelings with the child. There are several available. Try *Today I Feel* by Jamie Lee Curtis, *My Many Colored Days* by Dr. Seuss and *The Way I Feel* by Janan Cain. Give one of these books to him with a note that says, "All of your feelings are okay."

92.

TELL THE PARENTS' MARRIAGE STORY.

- Children can only deal with what they know. It's easier for them to confront their grief when they have a story to work with—a story with a beginning, middle, and end.

- If the child is unfamiliar with her parents' marriage story, don't be afraid to share it with her. Talk about the beginning (how her parents met, what they loved about each other, when they got married, and where they first lived). Then, let her tell you about the middle, what they were like together when she was younger and memories of times they got along and enjoyed each other. Walk through the ending with her and what got them to the point of divorce (without sharing unsuitable details). Give her the opportunity to understand this new ending while also knowing how it all began and how her parents' relationship unfolded across time.

CARPE DIEM

Look through the wedding album together. Let the child
ask questions and talk about what she sees in the photos.
Give her a copy of a wedding photo to keep.

93.

WATCH THE WEDDING VIDEO.

- Watch the parents' wedding video with the child. Watching the video can feel healing to him and help him piece together his parents' story, starting with Chapter One. It will give him a stronger sense of family to see how it began and how it progressed and help him integrate where the family is now, today.

- If you watch the video as a family, it might be emotional, with lots of comments and feelings, or it might be a solemn experience. Regardless, don't be afraid that showing the video or talking about the marriage will make him hold on to the idea of you two getting back together. Most likely, he is harboring that wish already. Try to keep your comments about the video positive or neutral.

- By watching the video, you're letting him know that it's okay to talk about the divorce, the wedding, and your marriage. It also shows him that you believe that it's okay to feel upset that the marriage is ending despite its beautiful start. Remember, your story is a part of the child's story—so it helps to remember it and reflect upon its past, present, and future.

CARPE DIEM

Let the child play dress up and pretend to have a wedding. It can be anyone's wedding—his, his parents, or a make-believe royal wedding between a frog king and a princess. Ask to join in.

94.

ENCOURAGE HER TO MOURN WITH EACH PARENT.

- It's important for kids to express their grief and pain to both parents. Doing so will help her fully integrate the divorce and avoid unfinished business later in life.

- As a parent, make a conscious effort to encourage your child to talk with your ex about her divorce grief. Rather than taking it as a personal complaint against you—as in, "I wish mom hadn't decided to move out"—see it for what it is—your daughter working through her pain.

- As parents, recognize that she needs both of you to hear her, right now. If she seems to talk more easily to your ex, set jealousy aside. Maybe she simply needs what your ex has to offer right now, and she'll come to you for something else.

- Both parents have something of value to offer their kids. Maybe dad helps lighten the mood with humor and mom is good at stopping everything and listening. Allow both of you to bring your strengths to the table to help your kids mourn. Resist dictating how each other acts as a parent. Rather, put your energy into sharing your own strengths.

- As a caregiver, help create opportunities for the child to spend time with each parent one-on-one.

CARPE DIEM

Get a package of markers and two pieces of paper.
Encourage the child to draw a picture of herself with
each of her parents teaching her something about divorce.
Ask her to tell you the story behind each picture.

95.

EXPECT GRIEFBURSTS.

- Don't be surprised if the child cries or has outbursts of emotions in unexpected places or at unforeseen times. He's having a "griefburst"—a normal reaction to grieving.

- If he has a griefburst, resist suppressing it or telling him to stop. Instead, step aside and give him a chance to feel what he's feeling and compose himself. If needed, change your plans—even if it means leaving an event.

- Sometimes, griefbursts disguise themselves as something else. He might act upset about not getting a toy that he wants in the store or getting to have a candy bar. See it for what it is. It might simply be easier for him to express his grief under the guise of something else.

- Most likely, having a griefburst will leave him feeling out of sorts. Tell him it's normal to have griefbursts during times of change and loss and that the best way to deal with them is to simply feel them and let them run their course. Offer reassurance and hugs.

CARPE DIEM

Give the child a candle to light (with the supervision of a grown-up) in memory of his family. For many kids, getting divorced feels like their family has died. Choose a candle that has a special significance by virtue of its shape, fragrance, or color. Attach a brief note and share your favorite memory about his family before the divorce. Letting him mourn this loss is an important part of healing.

96.

FACE THE PAIN.

- When we are in emotional pain, it can seem easier to ignore and avoid the pain than to confront it. Other people encourage us to ignore our feelings by telling us to stay busy and distract ourselves with constant activities.

- Doing some of this is a natural coping method to loss; we can only cope with so many emotions at one time. Yet if this is the primary way to cope with stress, grief, or pain, it becomes counterproductive. Denying our feelings only delays healing and invites emotions to come out sideways.

- By encouraging the child to keep busy and avoid his pain, you are encouraging him to move away from his pain. The only way to heal emotional pain is to wallow in the muck of it—explore it, recognize it, and learn how to best cope with it. Only then can we get to the other side of our pain. Pain that goes unexpressed simply lingers.

- Instead, encourage the child to look his pain straight in the eye— remembering that you need to let him guide you about when he's ready to do so, and how he wants to do it. Open the door by letting him know you are there for him if he ever wants to talk. Create opportunities through play, music, and outside time to invite that to happen.

CARPE DIEM

Today, spend time just being with the child. Do nothing.
Sit next to each other on the porch swing or park
bench and just be in each other's presence.

97.

REALIZE SHE'S LOST A PARENT.

- This may sound harsh—that the child has lost a parent—but it's true to some extent. Divorce changes people—how they act, feel, express themselves, and how much time they spend with their kids.

- Think about it. When parents divorce, kids lose time with each parent—where they used to see them both for a good portion of each day, now they see them separately for less time each.

- Besides losing time, the child loses emotional availability from both parents. She might also lose out on both parents being present at special events or during holidays. She also loses seeing her parents together, as a couple.

- It's important to recognize the ways she has lost connection with each of her parents.

- Help the child discover new ways of maintaining time with each parent and figuring out how to salvage some of the time that was lost. For example, instead of tucking her in each night, her mom can read her a story over the phone or say goodnight via a live computer video-cam.

CARPE DIEM

Assure the child that even though the family is now different, she can still rely on them for what she needs. Have her brainstorm ways she lost time with each individual parent since the divorce and find solutions for how to replace some of it.

98.

TAKE GRIEF OFF A SCHEDULE.

- Divorce grief lasts as long as it lasts. It's not a linear process that the child will go through. There are not stages or steps that he can take to cross over to acceptance and peace about the divorce. Rather, it's more circular. He'll cycle through common emotions associated with grief—denial, shock, anger, sadness, relief, acceptance, and others— versus walking through them in a straight line.

- When we're in grief our minds and hearts try to make the best sense of the situation we can in the moment. Sometimes, we feel hopeful and strong. Other times, we feel defeated and lost. The process through grief ebbs and flows with steps forward and steps backward. There's no set formula—everyone grieves differently.

- There is no timetable for the child's grief. Only he can determine—by what he feels and needs—what that journey will be like and how long it will last.

- You can help him through his grief process by accepting how he feels and encouraging him to express his feelings. By honoring his grief, even when it's inconvenient or disturbing, you'll be his companion in grief. In other words, you'll walk side-by-side with him, rather than leading the way.

CARPE DIEM

Give the child a calendar to organize his days, weeks, and months. Mark special dates—play dates, upcoming events, and special occasions like family birthdays and holidays. Have him mark when he's with each parent. Use different colored markers and stickers or stars to signify specific events, if desired. Ask if it's okay to mark the date of his parents' divorce so you two can have a ceremony next year to acknowledge the day.

99.

ESTABLISH "FAIR FIGHTING" RULES.

* One of the hardest things kids experience with divorce is watching their parents fight. That's because often during divorce, fights don't end with resolution. Rather than constructive conflict—where the goal is to discuss differences and come to resolution—destructive conflict involves aggression, name-calling, threats, cursing, crying, sulking, and the silent treatment. Witnessing these destructive behaviors is damaging to kids.

* When conflicts go unresolved, kids feel their parents' ongoing tension like an electrical current in their lives, keeping them on constant edge.

* On the other hand, some experts believe that it's okay for kids to see their parents fight—that is, if it's constructive conflict. When a child witnesses resolution, the fighting gives a lesson in compromise and how to work things out.

* Unresolved conflict between parents seeps into parent-child interactions and negatively influences parenting decisions.

* As parents, find a way to communicate with each other in a constructive way, even if you haven't come to terms with the divorce or why it happened. If needed, seek counseling to learn how to be in the same room with greater harmony.

* As a family, establish Fair Fighting Rules. Pick key behaviors that are off limits—and if one parent crosses the line, then the discussion must end immediately until frustrations and anger have cooled down. Make it a rule to not use the kids as go-betweens or as confidants when sharing frustrations about each other. Include the kids in the discussion of the Fair Righting Rules.

CARPE DIEM

Go to a public place and people-watch with the child. Point out examples of people in conflict, making notes on who is working out disagreements constructively and who is not.

100.

BE HONEST.

- Divorce is hard. As parents and caregivers we often want to make it better for kids. Yet the hard truth is that kids have to feel their pain. They have to grieve and mourn in order to get to the other side, where they can thrive despite the divorce.

- Instead of giving in to the temptation of saying, "It's going to be okay" when she cries, simply rub her back and let her know you know it's hard.

- Rather than trying to distract her from her pain by lining up non-stop events and activities, let her slow down so she can do the hard work of mourning.

- Resist the urge to give false promises, like: "I know the future will be great." Or "Things are going to be better than ever." To the child, she will always have lost something, no matter what else she gains along the way.

- Be honest. Admit that going through divorce hurts and that it's upsetting that the family has to change. Let her guide you on when she's done releasing her pain. You'll know she has crossed over when there's more room in her life for living and enjoying than for hurting and fretting. Think of her heart. When she carries grief in it, her pain and disappointment takes up a lot of it, with only a sliver left over to laugh and enjoy life. As she heals, her heart becomes a well of reception and can invite in joy, laughter, and connection again. There will be more room to experience a full, satisfying life.

CARPE DIEM

Have faith in the process of grief and mourning. Let the child know that she will not always feel the hurt she feels now.

A FINAL WORD

Thank you for making a conscious effort to help support children you know whose lives have been affected by divorce. As adults, it is easy to get caught up in the details around custody, financial decisions, and the emotional turmoil that parents express during divorce. It is all too common that we lose sight of the fact that divorce has a tremendous physical, cognitive, social, and emotional impact on children that reaches far beyond custody decisions.

When children are quiet about their experience or communicate that they are fine, it's what we adults desperately want to hear. The reality is that children are deeply affected by divorce even if they don't show it, and they need us to help them mourn the losses and hurt that they feel. If they get the help they need now, they are less likely to carry divorce grief with them as they move through childhood into adulthood. When children experience divorce, they often become what we refer to as "forgotten mourners." In our wish for them to be okay, it's easy to assume that it's true. Children, regardless of what they show us, need our love, encouragement, and support during the divorce and well beyond.

With the support of adults like you who understand that children feel grief when their parents divorce, children can go on to integrate their losses rather than let the losses weigh them down. When kids are able to reconcile the losses that come with divorce and make sense of all of the changes, they are better able to walk into their future. If they process their grief rather than suppress it, they are better prepared to cope with future loss and change, more able to give and receive love, and more likely to find authentic happiness.

We have both had the privilege of seeing children not only heal but grow through divorce grief. With the support of compassionate adults who companion them through their grief, kids of divorce emerge emotionally and spiritually stronger, more adaptable, and more able to appreciate life's gifts.

We commend you for taking on the challenge of companioning a child through grief after divorce. Your life—and the child's life—will be richer for it. Look to the future when you are faced with challenges and make the best decisions you can to help the child move through his or her pain. By taking on this noble job, you are giving the child the best gift you could ever give—a chance at a full, uninhibited life. Best wishes, and thank you for your courage, compassion, and desire to make a difference in a child's life.

THE GRIEVING CHILD'S
BILL OF RIGHTS

(Please share this with a grieving child you care about.)

1. **I have the right to have my own unique feelings about the divorce.** I might feel mad, sad, or lonely. I might feel scared or relieved. I might feel numb or sometimes not anything at all. No one will feel exactly like I do.

2. **I have the right to talk about my grief whenever I feel like talking.** When I need to talk, I will find someone who will listen to me and love me. When I don't want to talk, that's OK, too.

3. **I have the right to show my feelings about the divorce in my own way.** When they are hurting, some kids like to play so they'll feel better for a while. I can play or laugh, too. I might also get mad and misbehave. This does not mean I am bad, it just means I have scary feelings that I need help with.

4. **I have the right to need other people to help me with my grief, especially grownups who care about me.** Mostly I need them to pay attention to what I am feeling and saying and to love me no matter what.

5. **I have the right to get upset about normal, everyday problems.** I might feel grumpy and have trouble getting along with others sometimes.

6. **I have the right to have "griefbursts."** Griefbursts are sudden, unexpected feelings of sadness that just hit me sometimes—even long after the divorce. These feelings can be very strong and even scary. When this happens, I might feel afraid to be alone.

7. **I have the right to use my beliefs about God to help me with my grief.** Praying might make me feel better.

8. **I have the right to try to figure out why my parents got divorced.** But it's OK if I don't find an answer. "Why" questions about life are the hardest questions in the world.

9. **I have the right to think and talk about my memories of our family before the divorce.** Sometimes those memories will be happy and sometimes they might be sad. Either way, memories help me understand my past so that I can live and love in the present and the future.

10. **I have the right to move toward and feel my grief and, over time, to heal.** I'll go on to live a happy life, but the divorce will always be a part of me.

WANTED:
HEALING AFTER DIVORCE IDEAS

Please help us update the next edition of this book!

If an Idea is particularly helpful to you, let us know. Better yet, send us an Idea you have that you think others might find helpful. When you write to us, you are "helping us help others" and inspiring us to be more effective grief companions, authors, and educators.

Thank you for your help. Please write to us at:

Center for Loss and Life Transition
3735 Broken Bow Road
Fort Collins, CO 80526
Or email us at DrWolfelt@centerforloss.com or go to this website, www.centerforloss.com.

My idea:

_____

_____

_____

_____

_____

My name and mailing address:

_____

_____

_____

ALSO BY ALAN WOLFELT

Transcending Divorce
Ten Essential Touchstones for Finding Hope and Healing Your Heart

After years of being encouraged to contribute a book on divorce loss, Dr. Wolfelt has responded with this compassionate new guide. When it comes to grief and loss, divorce is one of the most heartbreaking for many people.

With empathy and wisdom, Dr. Wolfelt walks the reader through ten essential Touchstones for hope and healing. Readers are encouraged to give attention to the need to mourn their lost relationship before "moving on" to a new relationship.

If you're hurting after a divorce, this book is for you. Warm, direct and easy to understand, this is a book you will not want to put down.

ISBN 978-1-879651-50-0 • 195 pages • softcover • $14.95

Companion
PRESS

All Dr. Wolfelt's publications can be ordered by mail from:
Companion Press
3735 Broken Bow Road
Fort Collins, CO 80526
(970) 226-6050
www.centerforloss.com

ALSO BY ALAN WOLFELT

The Transcending Divorce Journal
Exploring the Ten Essential Touchstones

For many people, journaling is an excellent way to
process the many painful thoughts and feelings after a
divorce. While private and independent, journaling is
still the outward expression of grief. And it is through the
outward expression of grief that healing begins.

This companion journal to *Transcending Divorce* helps
you explore the ten essential touchstones for finding
hope and healing your grieving heart after divorce. Throughout, you will be
reminded of the content you have read in the companion book and asked
corresponding questions about your unique grief journey. This compassionate
journal provides you with ample space to unburden your heart and soul.

ISBN 978-1-879651-54-8 • 134 pages • softcover • $14.95

Companion
PRESS

All Dr. Wolfelt's publications can be ordered by mail from:
Companion Press
3735 Broken Bow Road
Fort Collins, CO 80526
(970) 226-6050
www.centerforloss.com

ALSO BY ALAN WOLFELT

The Wilderness of Divorce

Finding Your Way

This hardcover gift book is a compassionate, easy-to-read guide to finding your way through the wilderness of divorce. This book is an excerpted version of the comprehensive *Transcending Divorce: Ten Essential Touchstones*, making it a more concise, friendly guide for the newly divorced.

ISBN 978-1-879651-53-1 • hardcover • 128 pages • $15.95

Companion
P R E S S

All Dr. Wolfelt's publications can be ordered by mail from:
Companion Press
3735 Broken Bow Road
Fort Collins, CO 80526
(970) 226-6050
www.centerforloss.com

ALSO BY ALAN WOLFELT

Healing After Divorce

100 Practical Ideas for Kids

by Alan D. Wolfelt, Ph.D. and
Raelynn Maloney, Ph.D.

While divorce is common, it's also very difficult for
children, eliciting many challenging feelings. This book
for kids 7-12 gives them 100 simple ideas for expressing
their emotions during this life-changing time so that
they can go on to lead happy lives and develop healthy
relationships of their own.

ISBN 978-1-61722-138-5 • softcover • 128 pages • $11.95

Companion
PRESS

All Dr. Wolfelt's publications can be ordered by mail from:
Companion Press
3735 Broken Bow Road
Fort Collins, CO 80526
(970) 226-6050
www.centerforloss.com

ALSO BY ALAN WOLFELT

Living in the Shadow of the Ghosts of Grief

Step into the Light

Reconcile old losses and open the door to infinite joy and love

"Accumulated, unreconciled loss affects every aspect of our lives. Living in the Shadow *is a beautifully written compass with the needle ever-pointing in the direction of hope."*
— Greg Yoder, grief counselor

"So often we try to dance around our grief. This book offers the reader a safe place to do the healing work of "catch-up" mourning, opening the door to a life of freedom, authenticity and purpose."
— Kim Farris-Luke, bereavement coordinator

Are you depressed? Anxious? Angry? Do you have trouble with trust and intimacy? Do you feel a lack of meaning and purpose in your life? You may well be living in the shadow of the ghosts of grief.

When you suffer a loss of any kind—whether through abuse, divorce, job loss, the death of someone loved or other transitions, you naturally grieve inside. To heal your grief, you must express it. That is, you must mourn your grief. If you don't, you will carry your grief into your future, and it will undermine your happiness for the rest of your life.

This compassionate guide will help you learn to identify and mourn your carried grief so you can go on to live the joyful, whole life you deserve.

ISBN 978-1-879651-51-7 • 160 pages • softcover • $13.95

Companion
PRESS

All Dr. Wolfelt's publications can be ordered by mail from:
Companion Press
3735 Broken Bow Road
Fort Collins, CO 80526
(970) 226-6050
www.centerforloss.com

ALSO BY RAELYNN MALONEY

Waking Up

A Parent's Guide to Mindful
Awareness and Connection

by Raelynn Maloney, Ph.D.

This practical parenting guide by Dr. Raelynn Maloney
helps you become the parent you have always wanted to
be—one who is present, aware, and connected. Complete
with a series of simple Awareness Practices that help you
cultivate self, relationship, and moment awareness, *Waking
Up* will help you respond to your child in a healthy way and, in the process,
help her learn the value she brings into relationships with others.

In *Waking Up* you will discover how to:

- develop and consistently use awareness as an effective parenting skill.
- transform "problems" in the parent-child relationship by first transforming yourself.
- actively prevent the passing-down of negative relationship patterns.
- shift your child's mood, attitude, and behavior by focusing on the relationship instead of the child.
- become aware of the messages your child is taking in from you -- and to avoid sending back negative or mixed messages.
- become grounded in the present with your child — and to raise a child who is also capable of being grounded in the present.
- transform difficult situations and ordinary experiences into mindful moments.
- stay connected to your child during disagreements, when giving consequences, or while setting limits.

Imagine parenting without losing yourself in the drama, the debate, and the
tug of war. Interact with presence, openness, and confidence. Demonstrate the
skills, habits, and mindsets that will positively influence your child for life.

ISBN 978-1-61722-146-0 • softcover • 224 pages • $18.95

Companion
PRESS

All Dr. Maloney's publications can be ordered by mail from:
Companion Press
3735 Broken Bow Road
Fort Collins, CO 80526
(970) 226-6050
www.centerforloss.com